Francis Alÿs. The Nature of the Game

I0419123

Francis Alÿs.
The Nature of the Game

Edited by Gerard-Jan Claes and Stéphane Symons

Leuven University Press

Published with support of the KU Leuven Fund for Fair Open Access
and the KU Leuven Commission for Contemporary Art

Published in 2023 by Leuven University Press / Presses Universitaires de Louvain /
Universitaire Pers Leuven. Minderbroedersstraat 4, B-3000 Leuven (Belgium).

Selection and editorial matter © Gerard-Jan Claes and Stéphane Symons, 2023
Individual chapters © The respective authors, 2023

This book is published under a Creative Commons Attribution Non-Commercial
Non-Derivative 4.0 Licence.

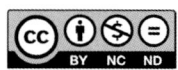

Further details about Creative Commons licences are available at
http://creativecommons.org/licenses/
Attribution should include the following information:
Gerard-Jan Claes & Stéphane Symons (eds), *Francis Alÿs. The Nature of the Game.*
Leuven: Leuven University Press, 2023. (CC BY-NC-ND 4.0)

Unless otherwise indicated all images are reproduced with the permission of the
rightsholders acknowledged in captions. The images are expressly excluded from the
CC BY-NC-ND 4.0 licence covering the rest of this publication. Permission for reuse
should be sought from the rightsholder.

ISBN 978 94 6270 384 1
e-ISBN 978 94 6166 541 6
D/2023/1869/29
https://doi.org/10.11116/9789461665416
NUR: 652

Layout: Theo van Beurden
Cover design: Daniel Benneworth-Gray
Cover illustration: Francis Alÿs, *Children's Game #10: Papalote*, Balkh, Afghanistan, 2011 (still)

Table of Contents

Preface

The KU Leuven Commission for Contemporary Art looks at the role of contemporary art for its research, education, and service to society as a world-class university. In this perspective we continue to develop a policy and strategy to acquire, show, discuss, and interact with contemporary artists and their artworks at the university. Within this context of science interacting with art and with society, we are convinced this leads to a synergy between scientific scholarship and artistic research.

KU Leuven's active presence at major artistic and societal initiatives includes its presence and support for the Belgian pavilion at the 59th Venice Biennale 2022. This participation demonstrates our commitment to connect scientists and artists in their combined research on complex societies.

The general theme of the Biennale addressed the question of how the definition of human is changing. This anthropocentric approach did not always result in optimistic visions of the future. The Belgian pavilion with Francis Alÿs's *Children's Games* distinguished itself in two ways. Children games are universal, in space and in time, and appeal to all of us as the fundamental nature of our humanity. Second, it probably was the only pavilion that conveyed hope and innocent joy.

With *Francis Alÿs. The Nature of the Game*, Gerard-Jan Claes and Stéphane Symons show how it is possible not only to 'walk the talk,' but also to 'talk the walk' of the nature of play. A multidisciplinary approach to children's games brings many university corners together, even when it requires out-of-the-box thinking, as was very clear in a preparatory seminar: from communication sciences to urban planning for playgrounds, from therapy to anthropology, from virtual reality to educational sciences.

I would like to thank Francis Alÿs, Hilde Teerlinck, and Jan Mot for their open-minded support in building the bridge between the arts and sciences. With this book, Gerard-Jan Claes (from the cinephile platform Sabzian and from the independent film distributor Avila) and Stéphane Symons (from the KU Leuven Institute of Philosophy) have contributed impressively to building that bridge. I am also grateful for the excellent collaboration between the WIELS Contemporary Art Centre (with its director Dirk Snauwaert) and KU Leuven, not to mention this common vision of museums and universities with regard to research in the arts and sciences. Finally, I would like to thank the entire Leuven University Press team for their professional way in merging scientific scholarship and art.

Geert Bouckaert
President of Leuven University Press
Chair of the KU Leuven Commission for Contemporary Art

Francis Alÿs. The Nature of the Game

Gerard-Jan Claes and Stéphane Symons*

I

Three title cards follow in quick succession: "Children's Games #1:" – "CARACOLES" - "Mexico City 1999." Then comes an initial image, which seems unframed, as if the camera is recording unintentionally. We recognize a street on which the sun casts a sharp shadow. Across the street, we see a man. A red pickup truck drives by, but even this vehicle does not provide any clue. Then a bottle rolls by, and the image suddenly comes into focus. The camera follows the bottle rolling down the steep street. A boy appears in frame. He kicks the bottle up the street, after which it rolls back down and he can start again. Here is the first cut in the montage. The camera is now behind the boy who kicks the bottle back up the road. Until it reaches a dog lying in the sun. The boy hesitates and looks at the cameraman, as if asking for help. The dog won't budge and snarls at the cameraman.

The video did not come about by chance. The cameraman clearly organized the situation and gave the boy instructions. Yet he also did not control everything. The street was not cordoned off for the filming; the scene is completely part of life in Mexico City.

* Gerard-Jan Claes is a filmmaker, lecturer, author, both the founder and director of the online cinephile platform Sabzian (www.sabzian.be) and co-founder of Avila (www.avilafilm.be), a film distributor and online video platform for Belgian cinema.

Stéphane Symons is Professor of Aesthetics and Philosophy of Culture at the Institute of Philosophy of KU Leuven, Belgium.

A new image shows a man with a bell crossing the street, with a glittering city in the background. We return to the bottle. The camera now coincides with the viewpoint of the playing boy. Francis Alÿs's *Children's Game #1: Caracoles* (1999), a short video of under five minutes, is not just a recording of an accidental moment. The 'scene' is set up and edited, re-filmed from different angles. Except for the dynamics of the editing, which mainly has a basic rhythmic function, little changes in the setup of the video itself. The premise remains basic: a boy enjoys himself kicking a bottle up a steep road. Until another dog clips the bottle in his mouth and runs away with it. Soon he drops the bottle, and the boy can continue. He kicks the object uphill again. When one of the kicks misses its target, the bottle rolls down the slope and the little film comes to an end.

Alÿs did not make this first little film with a whole collection of 'children's games' in mind. It connected with *El ensayo* (*The Rehearsal* (1999–2001)), a reflection on the notions of 'repetition' and 'rehearsal.' *Children's Game #2: Ricochets*, the second film in the collection, was shot eight years later. It is only in the following years that the project of the *Children's Games* was born, with a trip to Afghanistan as the main catalyst. Today, almost 20 years later, the collection counts more than 30 videos, each focusing on a single game. The concept is as straightforward as the title suggests: the collection presents the great diversity of children's games worldwide. For Alÿs, the *Children's Games* represent a seeming caesura with his previous work. Alÿs himself is no longer on view. The performative character so central to his earlier videos has here given way to a pervasive focus on the world in front of the camera. Yet the 'disappearance' of Alÿs is not a radical break and results in an intensified exploration of some of the guiding principles of his oeuvre.

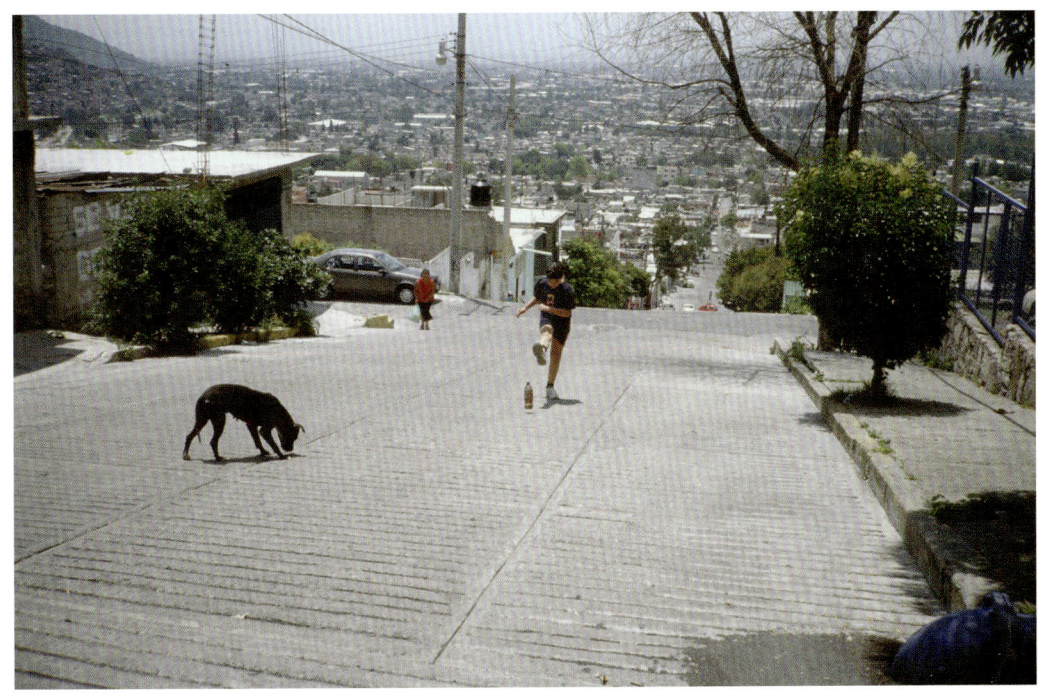

Francis Alÿs, *Children's Game #1: Caracoles*, Mexico City, Mexico, 1999 (still)

II

On first view, the 'goal' of the *Children's Games* seems uncomplicated: an inventory of children's games around the world. The project brought Alÿs and his team from Mexico to Afghanistan, from Belgium to Morocco, from the Democratic Republic of the Congo to Hong Kong. Even the presentation of the videos is conceived that way. They are carefully numbered, named after the game they document, and then brought together in exhibitions and on the artist's website. The collection did not end with the Biennale exhibition in Venice (2022), the exhibition at MUAC-UNAM in Mexico City (2023), or the exhibition at WIELS in Brussels (2023), all of which form the backdrop for this book. New videos are still being added to the collection. Systematically, with the resoluteness of a curator, Alÿs preserves bits and pieces of global heritage. In the Democratic Republic of the Congo, he absolutely wanted to document the *Kisolo* game, a 'count and capture' game that is at least 3,000 years old (*Children's Game #26: Kisolo* (2021)). It is a part of an immaterial heritage that is in danger of disappearing. It proved a difficult task to find children today who could still play the game. The current collection includes both globally known and lesser-known games. Usually, Alÿs looks for games that are connected to a particular place. For example, he films skipping rope in Hong Kong (*Children's Game #22: Jump Rope* (2020)), building sandcastles on the beach in Knokke-Le-Zoute (*Children's Game #6: Sandcastles* (2009)), playing marbles in Amman (*Children's Game #8: Marbles* (2010)), hopscotching in Iraq (*Children's Game #16: Hopscotch* (2016)), tossing in Nepal (*Children's Game #18: Knucklebones* (2017)), snow games in Switzerland (*Children's Game #33: Schneespiele* (2022)), and so on. Some games have a name and follow a set of fixed rules. In other games, children share the action with one or a few objects.

As an archivist, Alÿs's input remains at first glance rather minor. The games are recorded with a certain directness, without linguistic intervention, commentary voice, or informative captioning. We learn nothing about the cultural specificity or pre-history of the games. The videos are not manuals to instruct the viewer how the game is played. Yet they aim for a distinct transparency and readability. Unlike some of his earlier, acclaimed works (*Paradox of Praxis 1 (Sometimes Doing Something Leads to Nothing)* (1997), *Re-enactments* (2000), *A Story of Deception* (2003–2006), *The Green Line* (2004)), Alÿs does not assume the role of protagonist in the *Children's Games*. Nor does he engage with the children's games in an explicitly artistic manner. The mise-en-scène is modest, at the service of what takes place in front of the lens. The *Children's Games* are not technical feats but a collection of 'small' videos with limited 'production value.' Alÿs and his small team – a regular crew for years (Rafael Ortego, Julien Devaux, Félix Blume) – invoke tropes that could to a certain extent be described as 'amateur-like.' The rather small camera is hand-held, yielding shaky, searching imagery and a certain leniency towards technical glitches. This approach is obviously not the result of incompetence but of a deliberate relationship to what is being filmed. Alÿs records small, striking events and actions that take place in the small circle of a community and reports on his travels through his videos. For this amateur-like filmmaker, the camera is there for everyday use, less for a predetermined artistic purpose. Camera angles and editing rhythm are dictated by a concern to fully record and render the play in its intent. This desire to document asks for a direct, uncomplicated form. Thus, in a seemingly systematic manner, a worldwide archive of children's games takes shape.

This archival impulse is not in itself without risk because it can lead to superficial generalizations and a shallow form of humanism. In 1956, for example, the photographic exhibition *The Family of Man* landed in Paris, co-curated by the photographer Edward Steichen. The photographs presented, by 273 photographers from 68 countries, focused on the similarities that connect cultures around the world, as an expression of a restored humanism after the horror of World War II. A year later, Roland Barthes, in his *Mythologies* (1957), reproached Steichen for naturalizing humanity's behavior with his exhibition, labeling cultural and historical differences as secondary and accidental. In the show, 'man' is almost hypostasized into a divine abstraction and presented as a being that remains untouched by the course of history. Such facile poetics perpetuates for Barthes a false, sentimental impression of unity, which also immediately makes it impossible to explain how the horror of World War II had been possible at all. Against this "classical" humanism Barthes puts forward a "progressive" humanism, which starts from the realization that biological processes such as being born, dying, working, *and* playing always carry a historical dimension and are culturally variable. These aspects are crucial for Barthes. Only those who also put their finger on the differences that divide the human species from within can assume "that one can transform them, and precisely subject their naturalness to our human criticism."[1]

Alÿs escapes these facile generalizations and the sentimental humanism that might result from them. This achievement is in large part due to the distance he himself maintains, which makes the viewer primarily an observer as well. The road to empty identification is closed, and the children appear in a tangible environment that can be fundamentally *different* from that of the spectator. The *Children's Games* by no means show an ideal or idealized world in which everyone is fundamentally 'the same.' Rather, they reveal the extent to which cultural, geographical, and historical variables have an impact on and intersect with human behavior. This expression results in an exploration of the uniqueness of some games and the determining role of, for example, climatic conditions and urban development: no *Schneespiele* in Afghanistan, no *Kisolo* on the asphalted city squares in the West. The sum of the collection does not serve to erase differences, but points them out as "signs of an histori-cal writing" (Barthes). Alÿs's progressive humanism does not revolve around the observation that each individual, as a human being, contains a shared, essential core that relates them to all other individuals. It lies in the modesty of the act of observing and paying attention, which is always temporally and spatially anchored. Alÿs shows how people all over the world produce cultural products as a response to their specific living conditions. Play is not an expression of a purely natural process but an activity with, in many cases, delineated rules that people have agreed upon throughout history and which, at best, are passed down from generation to generation. By following these rules in their turn, the children inscribe themselves in these histories: they have learned these games and made the rules their own. They play the games that their parents, too, once played.

Alÿs seeks out the most diverse children's games and in this way re-draws the map of the world. Yet exactly what world does he allow to ap-pear here? Alÿs is not the artistic explorer from the West he is sometimes considered to be. He is not a globetrotter artist who constantly traverses the world and has become 'border-blind' in the process. And he does not put his work at the service of globalization, the 'universalization' of cultural traits, or the overcoming of histories. Alÿs's work does point out how the world is in danger of shrinking. Will children in the Democratic Republic of the Congo and Hong Kong soon all be playing the same games, on their smartphones or otherwise? The images of children's games created by Alÿs during his many travels call attention to a world that remains above all concrete and sensory, despite the equalizing dy-namics of globalization.

Through this cultural and historical perspective, Alÿs escapes the persistent tendency to glorify children. Often children are seen as 'ex-ceptional' beings with a natural innocence and spontaneous open-mind-edness. The child then becomes almost a *noble sauvage* who is in the antechamber of reality and not part of the 'real' world. The child would not (yet) be corrupted by civilization and would have a pre- or apolitical access to a more authentic, originary reality. In such a view, the child first and foremost needs care: it must be protected from the harsh world of adults. The blissful isolation by which the child remains somewhat immune to the outside world must be extended as long as possible. Not infrequently, this glorification of the child goes hand in hand with a glorification of the classic, mostly Western family structure and its customary gender roles. This glorification of the child and domestic safety underlies many well-intentioned artistic projects. Not only Steichen's *Family of Man*, but also explicitly socio-artistic photo series and portraits such as Jacob Riis's famous *The Children of the Poor* (1892) or Dorothea Lange's *Migrant Mother* (1936) essentially reduce the child to an object of care and protection and de facto isolate it from society.

The *Children's Games* distance themselves from this tradition of glorification. In doing so, unfortunately, there cannot always be blissful isolation for the child either. Many of the children in these videos face, and are even more vulnerable to, the same injustices that affect the adults in their communities. Alÿs thus puts his finger on the many forms of structural violence that make entire regions of the world unsafe today. In *Children's Game #19: Haram Football* (2017), Iraqi children are forced to play soccer with an imaginary ball because a real ball is banned by the fundamentalist regime in which they are growing up. In Mexico's Baja California and Ciudad Juárez, children play a shooting game with broken branches or shards of glass (*Children's Game #5: Revolver* (2009) and *Children's Game #15: Espejos* (2013)). Consciously or unconsciously, they mimic the violence of the drug cartels operating in those regions. Yet from the behavior of these children, wherever they are in the world, rings out *more* than an urgent call for care and protection. The *Children's Games* are above all a testimony to the resilience of children. In one of his notebooks, Alÿs makes this observation: "Through playing transform terror into mastery/control."[2] Indeed, the *Children's Games* bring out the specific form of action embedded in children's play. These children are not merely the object of care and protection but a very distinct subject of response and interaction. Moreover, in many of these games a community emerges that will not easily yield to traditional, pedagogical patterns or to the propensity of the classic, Western, self-reliant family for turning inwards. These children first and foremost need *each other* to play the game. Every game allows itself to be played only *together*, among children. Adults are here above all a disruptive, not a 'nurturing' or protective factor. Elias Canetti describes such a community as a "rhythmic mass," characterized by the desire to grow: "Man's feeling for his own increase was always strong." Unlike the traditional nuclear family, the "rhythmic" community of playing children is not self-reliant or inward-gazing but desires "large numbers."[3] In principle, these games are open to ever new, and different, participants. This creates a special situation: rather than a group of isolated individuals who encounter each other by virtue of certain *similarities*, the community of playing children is one of radical *equality*, and it is this way because everyone participates in the same activities. For this reason, children's play creates a space where society's codes of behavior, hierarchies, and gender roles may become visible but can be dealt with somewhat more freely.

In this community of 'equal' and playing children, then, it is striking that the center of the action often shifts from the individual children to the interplay of their bodies or, more precisely, their body *parts*. In many cases, the game revolves around a specific encounter of bodies and an interaction of limbs (*Children's Game #11: Wolf and Lamb* (2011), *Children's Game #14: Piedra, papel o tijera* (2013), *Children's Game #20: Leapfrog* (2018), *Children's Game #21: Hand Stack* (2019), *Children's Game #24: Pandemic Games* (2020), *Children's Game #25: Contagio* (2021), *Children's Game #28: Nzango* (2021)). Therefore, many games do not even require a prop. In Canetti's words, in a "rhythmic mass," it is important that [all members] should all do the same thing. They all stamp the ground and they all do it in the same way; they all swing their arms to and fro and shake their heads. The equivalence of the dancers becomes, and ramifies as, the equivalence of their limbs. Every part of a man which can move gains a life of its own and acts as if independent, but the movements are all parallel, the limbs appearing superimposed on each other. They are close together, one often resting on another, and thus density is added to their state of equivalence. Density and equality become one and the same.[4]

Perhaps the playing children in *Children's Game #28: Nzango* are the finest example of such a "rhythmic mass." In this Congolese game, which has become a national sport, participants imitate and anticipate the movements of each other's legs. Its rhythm is indicated by the unison singing and clapping of the bystanders. The video that Alÿs made with Rafael Ortega, Julien Devaux and Félix Blume begins with a solitary child staring in front of him in a sandy plain. Slowly, a group of children gathers around him and a beautiful choreography of dancing bodies unfolds. The video ends with close-up images of rhythmically moving lower legs and feet so attuned to each other that they almost seem to belong to one and the same body. The magic of the play lies in each individual child gradually being immersed into a larger whole.

Much more than Steichen's series or the social-artistic work of Riis or Lange, it is the oeuvre of American photographer and filmmaker Helen Levitt (1913–2009) which constitutes one of the artistic precursors of the *Children's Games*. In 1948, she wandered the streets of East Harlem, New York, with her camera to shoot the film *In the Street*. We see adults with dogs and mothers with strollers but, above all, children playing and dancing as they toy around with materials they find on the street: old socks are filled with sand and stones, newspapers and cardboard boxes are used as dress-up clothes and hats, a fire hydrant rigged up as a water sprinkler provides much needed cooling. The adults standing by don't take too much notice of these frenzied, interlocking bodies until one of them intervenes and stops the game. Levitt prefaces her film with an artistic statement that could just as well apply to Alÿs's project: "The streets of the poor quarters of great cities are above all a theater and a battlefield. There, unaware and unnoticed, every human being is a poet, a master, a warrior, a dancer and in his innocent artistry, he projects, against the turmoil of the street, an image of human existence. The attempt in this short film is to capture this image."[5]

III

As one expects of a lyric poet.
We look at the world once, in childhood.
The rest is memory.
— Louise Glück

In one of his books on cinema, Gilles Deleuze distinguishes two notions of childhood. On the one hand, there is the obvious, "horizontal" notion, in which childhood refers to a certain stage of life that passes irrevocably: "the horizontal succession of presents which pass outlines a route to death."[6] A memory of that lost phase is like an "image" of the past coming back to life. Such a memory is accompanied by the sweet mix of joy and sadness that we usually call 'nostalgia.' In addition, according to Deleuze, there is a "vertical" notion that associates childhood with a surprising "coexistence" and "simultaneity" between past and present. In such a notion, childhood is not merely a stage of life that we must one day irrevocably leave behind. Here childhood represents an exceptional view of the world that remains intact and accompanies us throughout our adult lives: "the child in us … is contemporary with the adult, the old man and the adolescent."[7] Remembering this particular perspective of the child does much more than merely revive an "image" of the past, however pleasant such a nostalgic experience may be. According to Deleuze, the second, "vertical" notion of childhood revolves around a memory that remains "pure": for a moment, our childlike view of the world actually returns in its fullness, and we realize that we had mistakenly considered it lost. "It is not in the recollection-image but in pure recollection that we remain contemporary with the child that we were as the believer feels himself contemporary with Christ."[8] The *Children's Games* are rooted in this second, "vertical" notion of childhood. These videos are primarily meant to be viewed by adults, but many of them retrieve from these short films an unexpected sense of rejuvenation, as if the child they once were has resurfaced for a very brief moment. That feeling cannot be fully captured by the term 'nostalgia' because it is much more immediate and, indeed, "pure." The *Children's Games* remind us of our own childhood, but they have nothing to do with the sense of lack and the awareness of loss that lie hidden in nostalgia.

So what exactly does this childlike perspective that seems to resurface ever so fleetingly consist of? And why might watching children at play be important for a "pure" memory of our childhood? In the *Children's Games*, Alÿs brings to view how the temporal dimension of childhood is linked up with a spatial dimension. Indeed, in many of the *Children's Games* the children interact not only with each other and each other's bodies or body parts but also with their immediate environment and with the many objects, small animals, and materials they retrieve within it. For example, the children make small holes in the ground and play a game with haphazardly found seeds (*Children's Game #26: Kisolo*). Small pieces of wood serve as revolvers or fence off a miniature playing field for shooting marbles (*Children's Game #5: Revolver*, *Children's Game #27: Rubi* (2021)). Stones are the material of choice for skipping across a body of water, playing a hopscotch game, or tossing (*Children's Game*

#2: Ricochets, Children's Game #16: Hopscotch, Children's Game #18: Knucklebones). A bottle, a bundle of leaves, or snow can be used as a ball, and sand can be used to make a sandcastle (*Children's Game #1: Caracoles, Children's Game #17: Chunggi* (2017)*, Children's Game #33: Schneespiele, Children's Game #6: Sandcastles*). Grasshoppers, in turn, are launched into the air like helicopters, mosquitoes outsmarted with an ingeniously mimicked sound, and snails deployed as racing vehicles (*Children's Game #9: Saltamontes* (2011), *Children's Game #30: Imbu* (2021), *Children's Game #31: Slakken* (2021)). Out of an old tire, these children manage to make a rolling toy or a vehicle (*Children's Game #7: Stick and Wheels* (2010), *Children's Game #29: La roue* (2021)). So it is almost as if the children in these games have made a mysterious pact with the place they are in. For a moment, it seems, the world presents itself to them just as they had desired it. These children find exactly the object or material they needed. Things become keys to the world. Furthermore, apparently the children have even unlocked one of nature's secrets, for the animals, too, now readily comply with the rules of their game.

That surprising alignment with the place in which the children live makes the *Children's Games* akin to fairy tales and fables, despite the references to all-too-real injustice and violence. Authors such as Walter Benjamin, Alexander Kluge, and Hans Blumenberg have pointed out that the core of fairy tales and fables can be found in a shrewd relationship to elements of nature. In contrast to myths, which typically feature the hubris of heroes and the antagonism between man and nature, the protagonists of fairy tales and fables no longer want to dominate or control their environment. Walter Benjamin describes it as follows: "Reason and cunning have inserted tricks into myths; their powers cease to be invincible. Fairy tales are the traditional stories about victory over these forces."[9] Through ruses, the main characters of fables and fairy tales make sure that their environment will come to their help when needed. They see nature as a possible ally that can strengthen their abilities at critical moments, rather than as an enemy to be feared. Alÿs has long been fascinated by this power of fables and fairy tales and by the possibility that the material things that surround us can help us out of trouble at crucial instants. In the performance *Fairy Tales* (1995), he wandered through Mexico City in a sweater that gradually unraveled due to a single thread that had come loose. With a nod to the story of Hansel and Gretel, he thus left a trail that would allow him to orient himself in the city chaos, and as with Penelope, the unwinding of a garment marks an ever-repeated moment of hopeful delay and respite. The performance was accompanied by the statement: "Whereas the highly rational societies of the Renaissance felt the need to create utopias, we in our times must create fables."

In the *Children's Games*, *La roue* is one of the finest examples of this fairy-tale pact between people and things. In this video, a Congolese boy first painstakingly pushes a tire up the hill only to crawl into it and roll down at dizzying speed. It is replete with references to the mythical hero Sisyphus, who twice sought to overcome death and as punishment had to keep pushing a rock to the top of a mountain only to see it roll back down time and again. *La roue*, however, is nothing less than an annulment of this ancient Greek myth. Unlike Sisyphus, the Congolese boy of *La roue* has managed to join forces with the object that initially cost him so much effort: when he swiftly descends the hill after his long climb, it is precisely that heavy, rubber tire that gives him the pleasure of play he had been seeking all along. Moreover, *La roue* also addresses the essentially *modern* myth that man is lord and master of nature and can dispose over it as he pleases. The hill on which the boy plays is in reality a pile of waste from a mine, thus constituting tangible evidence of the plunder of natural resources and child labor. The playing child transforms precisely this place of exploitation and injustice into a vast space for play. In this video, nature is no longer an 'outside' to be dominated and controlled but a participant in the game.

Such a pact with the place in which the children live does not come about for no reason, of course. If the world gives these children just what they need, it is because the children, in turn, know how to value that world and give it its due. For the children in the *Children's Games* literally anything can be made of use in play. They do not elevate themselves above things or pass judgment upon them. For them, there is no essential difference, let alone a hierarchy, between objects that have cultural or social significance and trash or goods that have become unusable. Benjamin also pointed out that children are

> irresistibly drawn by the detritus generated by building, gardening, housework, tailoring, or carpentry. In waste products they recognize the face that the world of things turns directly and solely to them. In using these things, they do not so much imitate the works of adults as bring together, in the artefact produced in play, materials of widely differing kinds in a new, intuitive relationship. Children thus produce their own small world of things within the greater one.[10]

In the "small" world that opens up in play, the opposition between the children and things is no longer essential. Alÿs therefore records the children in the same way as the objects they use. In *Caracoles*, the bottle receives as much attention as the little boy who kicks it up the hill. In *La roue*, the tire and the boy's body are not hierarchically set apart: Alÿs shows us how the boy's body folds to the curvature of the tire rather than vice versa. In *Children's Game #10: Papalote* (2011), we see how the gestures of kite-flying come about partly at the behest of the kite in the air: they are not merely the result of the Afghan boy's actions. In his discussion of children's intense "alertness" to "surrounding things," the French filmmaker, poet, and educator Fernand Deligny already pointed to the desire of children to become themselves a thing among things.[11] Children want to merge into the world. In this way, they do away with a purely practical and efficiency-oriented attitude. Deligny distinguishes between two forms of activity: the *faire*, which aims at productivity and efficiency and is organized according to a means-end rationality, and the *agir*, which has no goal in itself and accomplishes nothing essential. We find a key example of *agir* in Deligny's desire to be able to capture the endlessly slow melting of an iceberg on pellicule: "[H]ow much time that takes, this mass of which there will be nothing left but an ice cube, first the size of a fist, then nothing at all; nothing more than the sea."[12] Play clearly belongs to the category of *agir*: after all, play has no proper, practical use and is primarily a response to the many possibilities that lie embedded in our immediate environment. The games from the *Children's Games* are located somewhat outside our everyday activities. They cannot be fully absorbed by the consideration for usefulness and efficiency that is dominant in day-to-day existence. The type of children's game that Alÿs documents often consists of a set of rules that indicate a goal to be achieved and delineate the means and objects that can be used to that end. Even so, that goal is in fact only an improper part of a game, because it is the very success in a game which immediately brings it to an end: it *leads to nothing*.

Nevertheless, play is oftentimes a monomaniacal activity that is taken extremely seriously. When children play they can be completely immersed in their game. Play provides a zone of concentration where relationships and the interdependence of people, bodies, body parts, objects, materials, and even small animals are established purely on the basis of a set of agreed-upon rules. Without those rules, which seem to be of no value in the world outside the game, the game does not exist. Take away the rules, and the reality that founds the game goes up in smoke. That concentration and demarcation isolate the players from everything that does not belong to the space for play. They constitute a trait that play shares with fiction, which equally refers to a very distinct and different 'world within the world.' Like fiction, play is governed by a certain, independent logic and by a set of fundamentals that dictate laws.

These are 'made up' in all aspects (Latin: *fingere*: form, shape) and thus should, in theory, remain without direct consequence in the real world. Children at play create geographies with fictitious boundaries and demarcations: behind the couch begins the sea, and so as a participant in the game you are not to go there. Still, the frenetic reaction of children when you carelessly cross those imaginary lines already indicates that the internal 'emptiness' of the game does not prevent it from creating a reality. Break the rules of the game, and you transgress the prevailing laws of a world, however imaginary these may be.

With the *Children's Games*, Alÿs is adding a new chapter to his voluminous oeuvre, even though they are nevertheless closely related to his earlier projects. The proper status of fictions and legends, along with the 'added' reality they can establish, plays a major role in his work, the most well-known project being the performance *When Faith Moves Mountains* (2002). The artist invited five hundred volunteers to the outskirts of Lima to collectively move a sand dune by a few inches. Back in 1997, moreover, he realized Deligny's thought experiment when he pushed a large block of ice through the streets of Mexico City until it had melted completely. He gave this performance the title *Paradox of Praxis 1 (Sometimes Doing Something Leads to Nothing)*. Perhaps the apparent purposelessness of *agir* can even be called the guiding principle of his oeuvre. Indeed, in the apparent insignificance of many of his early works, Alÿs was already establishing a renewed interaction with the world, including the trash and supposedly unusable objects that are an integral part of that world (*The Collector (Colector)* (1990–1992), *Housing for All (Vivienda para Todos)* (1994), *Magnetic Shoes (Zapatos Magnéticos)* (1994), *Seven Lives of Garbage* (1995), *Barrenderos (Sweepers)* (2004)). In this way, he opened reflection on modern dogmas such as efficiency and progress and the relationship between time and labor. These themes remain unquestionably relevant in the *Children's Games*, as they, too, mark an imbalance between the great effort of global travel and its result, the 'small' videos of children's games.

IV

Alÿs travels all over the world filming children's games. He films the same thing everywhere: children playing. In doing so, he emphasizes that the children's games initially came his way through chance encounters and that the videos are usually created in the wake of his other activities as an internationally oriented artist. The *Children's Games* are deceivingly uncomplicated. They oscillate between something and nothing, almost nonchalantly, as if they were *trouvailles*, 'ready-mades.' The artist retains a childlike attitude himself, as it were, and effaces himself as a maker. The films are so straightforward that they might seem to have little artistic merit: there is no sought-after beauty or pretentious stylization, no explicit 'message.' It is this attitude that makes Alÿs's oeuvre in general so elusive. Where is it really? Is it Alÿs's performances, even if most often there were no 'professional' spectators present there? Or is it the videos? Or are those mere registration?

This straightforwardness opens a hunt for intentions and interpretations. The rudimentary form and 'down-to-earth' presentation of the small videos of children's games can even lead to a kind of distrust, compelling many to search for their 'meaning.' Yet the series has no secrets to give away. Alÿs essentially has nothing special to say. The appeal of the *Children's Games* results from how they bear witness to a specific response to the world. They are not created in support of this or that belief or conviction. Alÿs's gaze is attentive, not visionary. Such persistent attentiveness prescribes a certain aesthetic poverty. It results in a resistance to the artistic utility value that defines so much of contemporary art. Both at the level of the creative process and at the level of interpretation, the *Children's Games* traverse the expectations of many viewers. They resist both the anticipated virtuosity of the artist and the sought-after communicability of interpretations and meanings. Moreover, they are made available for free on the website, which makes for an interesting 'devaluation.' In a heated art market, exclusivity is fundamental for the work to retain a certain aura and (financial) value. Far from a conceptual masterstroke, this aesthetic poverty is above all the result of a desire for transparency and clarity. The French filmmaker Robert Bresson already distinguished two forms of artistic simplicity: as a "starting-point" and as an "end-product." Where the first is "sought too soon" and therefore remains vacuous, the second is the "recompense for years of effort."[13] For Alÿs, that second form is of great importance, as demonstrated in the animated film *Bolero* (*Shoeshine Blues*) (1999–2006). In this eight-minute film, we only see a hand polishing a shoe. Alÿs and his team worked on it for no less than eight years.

Iranian filmmaker Abbas Kiarostami, whose work is an important point of reference for Alÿs, also points out the difference between simplicity and dullness. He substantiates this with a story by Milan Kundera that greatly impressed him. Kundera describes how his father's lexical range narrowed with age, until at the end of his life only three words remained, which he kept repeating: "It's strange. It's strange."[14] Of course, this repetition does not mean that the man did not have anything to say anymore, but rather that he had reached the point where he could express an entire life with one single sentence. Perhaps, Kiarostami concludes, that convergence of simplicity and completeness is the true story behind minimalist aesthetics. This perspective was already behind Kiarostami's first short film, *Nan va Koutcheh* (*The Bread and Alley*) (1970). Kiarostami has called this short film "the mother" of all his films, not only because it was his first film, but also because in miniature form it foreshadows his full body of work. The first images show a boy kicking a can. He wants to go home but runs into an unfriendly-looking dog. Kiarostami thus presents narrativity in its most stripped-down form: a character wants to get from one place to another and stumbles upon an obstacle. Nothing more and nothing less. With Kiarostami, this trajectory has become both the content and the form of the film. For the film as well just moves from a starting point to an ending point. This movement is neither psychological nor plot-driven. Narrativity does not in this case revolve around a character following a complex, emotional trajectory, nor around a causal sequence of events, but around the meticulous recording of an unexpected moment of change. Indeed, in the end, the boy manages to overcome his fear, tempts the dog with a piece of bread, and then continues his walk *with* the dog. In terms of psychological development or plot structure, nothing extraordinary has happened, but by the end of the film, the child and his world have undergone a transformation: the antagonism between the child and the dog, with which the film had started, has now been undone and overcome in an uncomplicated manner. To effect this change nothing else was needed but a mere piece of bread.

The kinship with Kiarostami's pared-down narrativity goes far back into Alÿs's oeuvre. In 1996, Alÿs shot a video in Mexico City with the telling title *If You Are a Typical Spectator, What You Are Really Doing Is Waiting for the Accident to Happen*. In the video, the cameraman follows an empty plastic bottle that is caught by the wind, blown across a square, occasionally held up, and then continues its journey. The bottle has become the real main character in this film. The film bears many similarities to a late work by Kiarostami, *Five Dedicated to Ozu* (2003), which is composed of five long minimalist sequences filmed on the Caspian Sea, all focused on the water, almost without camera movement. In the first sequence, we watch a piece of driftwood on the shore being swept along by the waves and all but falling apart. *If you are a typical spectator, what you are really doing is waiting for the piece of wood to be smashed by the waves.* This work is Kiarostami's most radical attempt to present narrativity in its reduced form: there is nothing but set-up, anticipation, and outcome.

Kiarostami's cinema also exerted a particular influence on the *Children's Games*. Alÿs has even called this series an attempt to continue Kiarostami's artistic project.[15] In both the *Children's Games* and

Kiarostami's films, the objects partly escape human will. They are often propelled by chance or nature, and when it is man who sets them in motion, he can never unilaterally impose his rhythm on them. "You are my polo ball / running before the stick of my command / I am always running along after you, / though it is I who make you move," Kiarostami quotes the Persian poet Rumi.[16] *Caracoles*, the first installment of the *Children's Games* bears an obvious, visual resemblance to the opening images of *The Bread and Alley*, and in many of Kiarostami's other films, too, we see how things are carelessly set in motion by a variety of characters: in *Solution* (1978), someone rolls a tire down the highway; in the later *Close-Up* (1990), a spray can goes spinning when a man is kicking it down a steep road. Yet the affinities between Alÿs and Kiarostami are of a more fundamental nature. Alÿs, too, strips narrativity of the ballast of psyche and plot, so as to reduce it to its most basic building blocks. Thus each game can be seen as a specific trajectory to get from a start to an end point, doing so by means of clear rules and agreements that function as obstacles. Like Kiarostami, Alÿs wants above all to catch an unsuspected possibility of change. *Children's Game #23: Step on a Crack* (2020) is a wonderful illustration of this. A girl is making her way through the busy streets of Hong Kong, leaping with great strides over the yellow stripes of crosswalks and the joints of paving stones. There is no more to see here than a child moving from one place in the city to another, imposing a number of obstacles on herself. Yet this film, too, revolves around a renewed promise of transformation. With every step she takes, the girl skillfully detaches herself from the world and its limitations: for a split second, over and over again, her feet let go of the ground. Each yellow line or joint she jumps over marks a hurdle that can be taken almost carelessly. Thus *Step on a Crack* acquires a power of expression that extends far beyond its minimalist appearance. This video tells us as much about a girl at play as about the sense of opportunity, change, and possibility that pulsates along in the urban bustle of a metropolis.

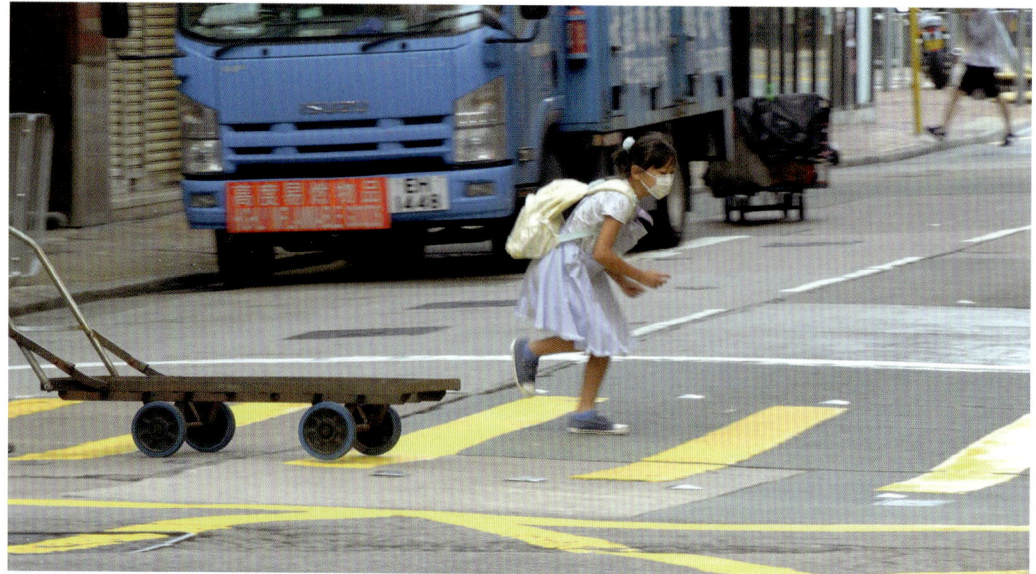

Francis Alÿs, *Children's Game #23: Step on a Crack*, Hong Kong, 2020 (still)

Francis Alÿs. The Nature of the Game

The medium of film occupies a special place in such pared-down narrativity. "Cinema's realist destiny – and its congenital photographic objectivity – is fundamentally equivocal," wrote French film critic André Bazin.[17] Through its photographic capabilities, film is 'of itself' a metaphor for reality. Indeed, the shot creates access to the real *and* distance from it at the same time. As a medium, it is a form of 'immediate' imagery: film is at once literal and figurative. It reflects the world but also re-produces it into and as something else, an *image*, with one and the same gesture. Perhaps it is therein precisely that lies the undeniable poetic and even social dimension of film, of Alÿs's oeuvre, and of the *Children's Games* in particular. The poetry of the series unfolds as a poetry of definition, a 'zero degree poetry.' It arises from the realization that the mere existence of the world should suffice for us to radically rethink it. In other words, there is no need to further burden the world with *meaning*. Rather than meanings or truths, Alÿs seeks a perspective that illuminates our environment, in one and the same moment, both as it *is* and as it *can become*. The child's gaze is above all that: a combined sense of proximity and distance which, without negating reality in its current shape, always also looks further. It makes us realize that *a window is required for whoever wants to retrieve a view of the world*. Perhaps that is the true, and only, place of a poetry that does not reveal meanings or truths but gives us novel eyes to experience the world and its possibilities. It is through this form of poetry that the world can be brought out as *changeable*. The Dutch poet Willem Jan Otten put it this way:

> Perhaps you had to say narratively what poetry is. For example: one December day in 2015, Christmas trees appeared in the Colombian jungle, along the path that led to the hidden headquarters of the terrorist movement FARC. Fully decorated Christmas trees, with angel hair, lights and a spike. With each Christmas tree was a sign: 'If Christmas can come to the jungle, you can come home. Put down

your weapons. At Christmas, anything is possible ...' From this example (which explains that a poem does not necessarily have to be of language) it can be seen that a definition of poetry, especially if it is narrative, can have the character of a creed, you profess that this – Christmas trees in the hostile jungle – is 'it'. These poems (Christmas trees) I believe.[18]

A passage from Walter Benjamin's autobiographical essays makes us understand why such a form of poetry is indeed linked to childhood and the activity of play. He describes how as a small boy he became fascinated by an extremely banal piece of clothing, a rolled-up stocking, and could not get enough of putting his hand into it as deeply as possible. Again and again he was overcome by the expectation that there was "a little present" hidden inside the stocking. Of course, each time the stocking was unrolled, it turned out that nothing was hidden within it. For Benjamin, though, this moment was by no means disappointing. For it was precisely the unexpected transformation of "a little present" into an ordinary stocking that provided him with the pleasure he was looking for. Indeed, that surprise meant that the stocking itself could now be received as a kind of "present." "I drew (the anticipated 'little present') ever nearer to me, until something rather startling would happen: I had brought out 'the present,' but 'the pocket' in which it had lain was no longer there. I could not repeat the experiment on this phenomenon often enough."[19] The little game with the stocking made Benjamin realize that the most insignificant things can be the site of unannounced metamorphoses and innovations. According to him, this experience is characteristic not only of "poetry," but also of childhood. Children feast on the mere there-ness of things by drawing from them an unexhausted potential. This allows for pure presence to be experienced as 'sufficient,' and it cancels out the longing for radically different things or faraway places. "(R)olled up in the laundry hamper, (the stocking) is a 'bag' and a 'present' at the same time. (C)hildren do not tire of quickly changing the bag and its contents into a third thing – namely, a stocking."[20]

In such an experience, the world as a whole offers itself to us as accessible but also 'new.' It is this primarily poetic yet multifaceted interaction with the world around us that we find at the heart of the *Children's Games*. They have traded the search for extraordinary meanings or deep truths for a sensitivity to *repetition*. The children's games in Alÿs's videos revolve around certain actions and gestures that in most cases are unremarkable but can, and should, be repeated. From the bottle that is kicked up the hill over and over again in *Children's Game #1* to the snowy descents in the recent *Children's Game #33*: these children perform the same activity time and again, but the surprise effect and joy remain undiminished. These repetitions go hand in hand with a sense of temporality. Even the most enjoyable play must at some point come to an *end*. The children are tired – or are tired *of it*. An argument breaks out, or an adult brings the game to a stop. These interruptions, however, are never final: a game demands to be played over and over again. Children are driven by the desire to invest time again and again with new but identical actions that enable the activity of play as such to remain unexhausted.

This combination of ephemerality and repeatability is duplicated at the level of the medium of video. Unlike paintings, sculptures, or buildings, the duration of a video is unavoidably interrupted and limited in time. Alÿs not only meticulously specifies the duration of each *Children's Game*, but the loops in which the videos are viewed, too, cannot but come to an end at some point. At the end of the day, the LED screens in the exhibition space are turned off one by one, and after watching a number of *Children's Games*, we close our laptops. The next day, though, the LED screens come back on and our laptop goes back open, and it appears that the videos have undergone no change whatsoever, as if they have become detached from the passage of time. This inability to *endure* or, expressed positively, the ability to be *repeated*, is essential to both the children's games and the *Children's Games*. It brings with it an unmistakable fragility. After all, the existence, and survival, of these games, and of these videos, depends entirely on the children who keep repeating them, and on us who keep watching the videos. As a result, both these games and the videos are permanently threatened with extinction. Even so, the repeatability of these games and videos reveals a stubbornness and persistence as well. They manage to thrive on the frayed edges of a globalized world, nestling comfortably within the vast amount of footage that races through the ether at all instants.

Notes

1. Roland Barthes (2000). "The Great Family of Man." In *Mythologies*. Trans. Annette Lavers. London: Vintage. 101.

2. 59th Biennale di Venezia (2022). *Francis Alÿs: The Nature of the Game*. Berlin: DCV Verlag.

3. Elias Canetti (1988). *Crowds and Power*. Trans. Carol Stewart. London: Phoenix Press. 31.

4. Ibid. 32.

5. Helen Levitt, *In the Street*, see https://www.youtube.com/watch?v=hznvV2bBkX4&t=1130s

6. Gilles Deleuze (1989). *Cinema 2. The Time-Image*. Trans. Hugh Tomlinson and Robert Galeta. Minneapolis: University of Minnesota Press. 91.

7. Ibid., 92.

8. Ibid., 91–92.

9. Walter Benjamin (1999). "Franz Kafka. On the Tenth Anniversary of His Death." In Michael W. Jennings, Howard Eiland, and Gary Smith (eds.). Walter Benjamin. *Selected Writings. Volume 2. Part 2. 1931–1934*. Cambridge, MA: Harvard University Press. 799.

10. Walter Benjamin (2004). "Old Forgotten Children's Books." In Marcus Bullock & Michael W. Jennings (eds.). Walter Benjamin. *Selected Writings. Volume 1. 1913–1926*. Cambridge, MA: Harvard University Press. 408.

11. Fernand Deligny (2017). "Les détours de l'agir ou le moindre geste." In Sandra Alvarez de Toledo (ed.). Fernand Deligny. *Oeuvres*. Paris: L'Arachnéen. 1290. See also Fernand Deligny (2017). "Singulière ethnie". In *Oeuvres*. 1472.

12. Fernand Deligny (2017). "Camérer." In *Oeuvres*. 1743.

13. Robert Bresson (1950–1958). *Notes on Cinematography*. Trans. Jonathan Griffin. New York: Urizen Books. 36.

14. Abbas Kiarostami (2002). "Kiarostami on Ten." Retrieved May 5, 2023 from https://zeitgeistfilms.com/media/films/89/presskit.pdf.

15. See the interview that is included in the present volume (p. 49).

16. Kiarostami, interviewed by Mehrnaz Saeed-Vafa and Jonathan Rosenbaum. In Mehrnaz Saeed-Vafa & Jonathan Rosenbaum (2003). *Abbas Kiarostami. Expanded Second Edition*. Urbana, IL: University of Illinois Press. 72.

17. André Bazin (1947). "Every Film is a Social Documentary." Trans. Sis Matthé. Retrieved on May 6, 2023 from https://www.sabzian.be/text/every-film-is-a-social-documentary. Also included in Hervé Joubert-Laurencin (2018) (ed.). André Bazin. *Écrits complets*. Paris: Macula.

18. Willem Jan Otten (2022). *Wil je mij poëzie leren?*. Amsterdam: Uitgeverij Van Oorschot. 27. Trans. authors.

19. Walter Benjamin (2002). "The Sock." In Howard Eiland & Michael W. Jennings (eds.). Walter Benjamin. *Selected Writings. Volume 3. 1935–1938*. Cambridge, MA: Harvard University Press. 374. Trans. modified.

20. Idem. (1999). "On the Image of Proust." In Michael W. Jennings, Howard Eiland & Gary Smith (eds.). Walter Benjamin. *Selected Writings. Volume 2. Part 1. 1927–1930*. Cambridge, MA: Harvard University Press. 240.

Interview with Francis Alÿs and Rafael Ortega, Nov. 9, 2022

Gerard-Jan Claes and Stéphane Symons

I

A few days prior to conducting this interview we wrote a short introductory paragraph about the *Children's Games* as a way to prepare ourselves. We sent it to Alÿs and his collaborator Rafael Ortega beforehand:

> The beautiful but also immediately difficult thing about your *Children's Games* is that it is very hard to talk about them. The magical quality of the work is that it holds no secrets. It's dazzlingly direct, 'it's all there is.' At the same time, that clarity is deceptive. The videos sometimes seem like nothing more than *trouvailles*. But, of course, this is not the case. With this interview, we want to get a clearer view on how these videos came about, regarding pre-production, production, and post-production.
>
> We will therefore not be asking questions about possible interpretations and underlying intentions. Not only because we know you do not generally like these questions but also because we think the question about the 'meaning' of these videos, or about the 'meaning' of a game, is ill-conceived. We regard these videos, and the games

they document, as powerful, not because they convey certain ideas, not even because they testify to the supposed powers of imagination, but because they embody a specific way of interacting with
the world. The strength of the series is the fact that these games are
shown to be, to a certain extent, 'without any meaning or intention.'
We want to avoid clichés about the so-called pedagogical value of
playing since we consider that playing has no instrumental value,
properly speaking. Playing does not really teach us anything except
what Michael Taussig has called 'the mastery of non-mastery,' that is,
the sustained, deeply human reaction to things that will not ever be
fully controlled.[1] These videos and the games they document indicate
for us first and foremost a specific response to very specific objects,
landscapes, and environments. We want to take their embodied and
material quality seriously and will therefore not be fishing for artistic
statements.

II

Francis Alÿs: I very much liked the introductory text. I mean, you said
it all.

Stéphane Symons: Perhaps, then, we can start by going back to
the origins of the project. Was it clear from the first video onwards
(*Children's Game #1: Caracoles* (1999)) that this would be a long-term
project? Was it a planned shoot? And did you already know from the
outset that this would be part of a collection of documented games that
would be multiple years in the making?

Alÿs: Back in 1999, it was a planned shoot in as far that it was a re-
make of a scene I had seen a few days earlier in that same neighborhood
in the outskirts of Mexico City, where my collaborator Emilio lives. At

the time, I was working on the 'mechanics of rehearsal,' with Rafael as it happens. The main film we were working on involved a small red Volkswagen going up and down the hill, responding to the rehearsal session of a band from Juchitán (*Rehearsal I (El Ensayo)* (1999–2001)). And the other film was a striptease scene which was produced in a strip club in New York City a bit later (*Rehearsal II* (2001–2006)). Both were about Latin America's relationship to the concept of production and the dogma of efficiency; they were recalling the Latin American scenario in which modernity is always postponed. When I saw that boy kicking a plastic bottle up a hill, the scene had an immediate echo with the rehearsal films. But it was not at all thought of as the document of a children's game. That only came much later.

The next one, *Children's Game #2: Ricochets* (2007), was a scene we encountered with Rafael, this time on a beach in Tangier. A bunch of boys were skimming stones across the waves of the Strait of Gibraltar. Again, there was a very strong connection with the project we were working on (*Don't Cross the Bridge Before You Get to the River* (2008)), which was creating the illusion of a bridge with lines of children pushing little boats made with shoes from both sides of the Strait. Those littles stones wanting to reach the horizon were another illustration of the same story. The whole scene was filmed in fifteen minutes.

Rafael Ortega: The children we were working with started playing. While now they have a completely different structure, at the beginning these videos always came about through chance and observation.

Alÿs: Chance encounters.

Ortega: When Francis discovers games through such chance encounters, I always see them before the shoot, in drawings in a sketchbook. They have already been recorded in a graphical form rather than a filmic one. For example, when we did the video with the Volkswagen, we found certain points of connection. We created a maquette of the rehearsal of the Volkswagen with a camera and Francis went to this area of the city to look for a place where we could film. He then encountered the boy with the bottle. And so it bounced back one from the other.

While doing the project in Tangier, one of the kids who was very bored started picking up stones and throwing them. All of a sudden something happened. Francis started making drawings that had to do with this idea. We were already at work on the project of the bridge. This was like a symbolic bridge that was being built in the air.

Alÿs: Interestingly enough, the Gibraltar project was a turning point for me. It was my second attempt to build a bridge across different continents. We had done an earlier attempt between Havana in Cuba and Key West in Florida (*Bridge/Puente* (2006)). This time, the idea was to do a similar project across the Strait of Gibraltar, collaborating with the communities of fishermen of both African and European continents. This gave rise to extremely complex negotiations with local powers, which on the Moroccan side even went all the way to King Mohammed, who was about to open a new harbor next to Tangier and wanted to use our image of a bridge across the Strait as a sort of propaganda image. Our project was turning into something completely different. My disappointment with the response of the adults made me turn to the children of the beaches from both sides and ask them to become the protagonists of my project instead of the adults. And from there on, the children took over developing scenarios and assuming the protagonistic role in my projects.

But to get back to your earlier question, it was probably around that time that I took on the habit to film children's games, even though at first it was just a way of making contact with cultures I knew little to nothing about. The contemporary art world has this peculiar habit of inviting you to operate in contexts which are completely foreign to you. This was the case when Carolyn Barkiev invited me to Afghanistan in 2010, where I felt completely out of place. I started filming children playing on the street as a way to break the ice and try to find an entry point. Doing that also allowed me to gauge how people reacted to the presence of an outsider and to a camera. It's a sort of mutual observation process which allows me to learn fast about the local cultural codes and feel what can and cannot be done, which can go from the prohibition to film women to how you place your feet when you are sitting next to someone. From the trip to Afghanistan onwards, when I would arrive in a new location, the first thing I would do would be to ask to be taken to places where kids are playing, always in the open air and public spaces. That is where a relation might eventually start, simply by observing. In some cases it can lead to a project, like it did in Afghanistan, where the children excelled at the game of stick and wheels. *Children's Game #7: Stick and Wheels* (2010) inspired *Reel-Unreel* (2011), with the wheel simply replaced by a film reel. Of course, other elements feed the story, like the episode of the Taliban burning the national film archive. It is important to clarify that I was invited to all the places where the children's games were filmed. It was not a deliberate choice to go to, for instance, Sri Lanka to film a specific game. The filmings happened because I was invited to do a project somewhere, and that eventually led to the documentation of a local game. But game after game a project was taking shape.

Gerard-Jan Claes: There is a certain similarity between the various games. Most of the games deal with an object and a fixed set of rules. There are not a lot of games based on roleplay or forms of theater. Was that focus something you developed as the project progressed? Was there a certain point when it became clear what kind of games you were looking for? And which games you did *not* want to film?

Alÿs: At first, it was totally random. Wherever I would be invited in some unfamiliar context I would film children's games and whichever game I would encounter would enter the compilation. This sort of ethnological archive of shared experiences around the world seemed to build in significance with each new game and each new culture entering the series. I certainly favor games that can be made out of nothing, or out of anything that can be found on the site of the game, like a handkerchief, some pebbles, an empty can, … It's often about invention and adapting the context to the end of the game, like with the kids in Amman using old train tracks to delineate the boundaries of their marbles game. It is not an absolute rule but if there is a prop, it should be a simple one, like in jump rope (*Children's Game #22: Jump Rope* (2020)). In its first phase, the series was indeed essentially building upon chance encounters.

This has changed over the years. When I am invited somewhere now, I do some research beforehand and plan more ahead which games could best enrich the series. For example, when I was invited for the Lubumbashi Biennale in the Democratic Republic of the Congo, I really wanted to film the *Kisolo* game, a variant of the *Mancala* game, partly because it is one of the most ancient games surviving today – possibly as old as 3000 years – but also because it seems this game might come from that region of the world (*Children's Game #26: Kisolo* (2021)). Once there, I came across many unexpected games, like *Nzango* and the one with the tire (*Children's Game #28: Nzango* (2021), Children's *Game #29: La roue* (2021)). I ended up filming five other games over three visits. For three of them, it's actually the kids who pulled me by the sleeve to show me their favorite games.

Paradoxically, the more games enter the series, the more 'holes' appear. So far, very few games in the series play on words or receive their rhythm from rhymes. I can only think of *Rock-Paper-Scissors*, *Nzango*, and *Step on a Crack*. But, when seen together, games can also become the portrait of a society at a particular moment of its history, like Pieter Bruegel the Elder's *Children's Games* (*Kinderspelen* (1560)), a painting I saw as a child and which really made an impression on me. In my children's games compilation, I am opening up the series to a more global panorama because I think the extraordinary coexistence of similar games at opposite corners of the planet is a natural consequence of today's globalization. Whereas some games are still specific to a local culture, others have a more universal quality, like hopscotch or knucklebones.

Others can also be syncretic, when a culture adopts and adapts a game originally coming from another culture and creates its own version of the game. There are distinguishing and uniting elements in all games. I hope the series illustrates as much the singularity of cultures as the many transcultural aspects of childhood experience.

During the pandemic something fascinating happened to the very popular – and transcultural – game of *Chase Tag*, also called 'It.' In 2020, at the height of the spread of the virus all over the world, a game appeared in which the chaser was the virus itself or someone infected with it. The virus would be chasing the others players who would become infected when tagged. This adaptation of the classic tag game was reported in around fifty countries over the world. I was fortunate to document its Asian version in Hong Kong (*Children's Game #24: Pandemic Games* (2020)) and its Mexican version (*Children's Game #25: Contagio* (2021)). It is a fantastic example of how the act of playing can help children cope with traumatic experiences by turning the dramatic circumstances around them into a more fictional, ludic world.

What strikes me is that games are transmitted from one generation to another without any apparent volition. It just happens. Or happened. Because things are changing. Games that existed for centuries are becoming more difficult to encounter. *Kisolo* is a good example: the elders still knew how to play it, but it was not easy to find children that could still play *Kisolo*. My decision to focus more on the series now certainly has to do with that feeling of loss. Maybe the pandemic accelerated this phenomenon, or at least made it more obvious ... The compilation came from the desire to preserve a memory of a form of children's social interaction that is slowly disappearing, be it because of the omnipresence of cars in cities, because of the growing dependence of children on social media and digital entertainment, or because of the parents' concerns about the safety of their children in the public space. You name it ... Whereas children's games have been transmitted orally for centuries and in some cases thousands of years, today they are slowly being erad-icated from our way of life. I am not sure whether that is a good or a bad thing. It is not for me to judge, and it is too early to judge. But it is important to register that moment of transition. And there are still so many essential games which I would love to incorporate!

<h1 style="text-align:center">III</h1>

Symons: Can you explain to us how the videos are produced exactly? And how does your collaboration take shape?

Ortega: When we were doing *The Rehearsal*, Francis went to make *Children's Game #1: Caracoles* and asked me for a camera. He asked me for a wide-angle lens because he wanted to follow the boy around and film the scene himself. This was just something he tried to register one way or another. But Francis evolves in his moving-image language and rethinks his ways of creating it … he works on it. *Children's Game #2: Ricochets* was very much of the moment. We had been working closely together on the project in Tangier so he just told me to look at a particu-lar scene he encountered. We both jumped into that situation and kind of 'covered' the minimal aspects of the image …

Alÿs: … the 'essential' aspects.

Ortega: For *Children's Game #5: Revolver* (2009) we used a Super8 camera. Francis had some rolls of film, and he asked to use my camera. For me, *Children's Game #5: Revolver* is a very important piece. Unlike video, a roll allows you to film for only three minutes. I remember tell-ing Francis that he had to edit in the camera, while filming. Whatever he was filming, he had to run and cut. But that is something he already knew. *Children's Game #5: Revolver* is also a fascinating project because Francis started working on the language itself. For a collaborator, it is very interesting when it is clear what Francis is looking for. He has cer-tain questions to get to certain places but the original, seminal idea of the *Children's Games* was already there through drawings and photographs.

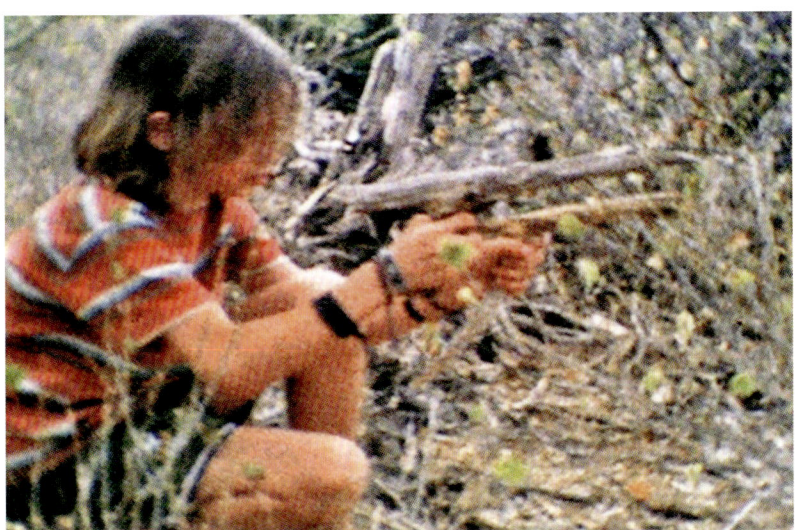

Francis Alÿs, *Children's Game #5: Revolver*, Baja California, Mexico, 2009 (still)

Alÿs: Some games are relatively straightforward. Others are quite complex. Before filming, we need to fully understand the mechanics of each game. What is the role of each player? What rules are there to organize the interaction? What is the goal of the game, if there is one? Is it a mixed-gender game? In most cultures, games are the first moment of gender separation. Through this preparation, we know which information we will need to capture in order to build a clear narrative during the editing process, one that will allow the viewer to understand the game without the help of written information. With the first images we try to give the viewer a hint of where the games take place, in what part of the world. This cancels out unnecessary questions and helps the viewer enter the game faster. No matter how good or bad we film, all those components have to be present. Maybe this is what makes them different from the many videos of games one can find online. In our videos the games are self-explanatory.

Ortega: Throughout making the small films – small in terms of duration and production – certain rules have been developing themselves. There is no use of props. However beautiful the image may be, it is useless if it does not help you to understand the game. At the end of the film, you need to have a general overview. You need to somehow understand why, for instance, a participant has an advantage over someone else when he has an object and the other person hasn't. You have to understand the rules of the game. And the games do not happen nowhere. They always happen in a specific place, which has to be part of the film. This place needs to be 'described' one way or another and comes with its own set of rules. It is a completely different 'ball game,' as they say, if you are filming kids who are nine or twelve years old, or if you are filming two kids in the company of twenty-four kids who are of all ages.

Symons: Are the preparatory drawings like storyboards? Do you already anticipate the angle of the camera and the editing of the videos?

Alÿs: No, drawing can be a way to prepare myself, but it rarely addresses the games themselves. As you and Gerard-Jan put it in the short text you sent us, the magical thing about a game is that it's all there is. If anything, the drawings or small paintings I may do on location depict the context in which the games take place. If they were made before the visit, they are rather meant to create a sort of mental build-up before the rush of the filming. Because of my present family situation, I cannot travel for months. I travel for short periods. When I arrive, I have to be prepared, already emotionally connected with the place and my local partners. I need to be ready to jump in. And once the game is launched, it's the children who are in charge of the script. We are just reacting and adapting to the choreography of their play.

Recently, we made a film in Copenhagen with very young kids dancing in couples, holding an orange between their little foreheads. It is a very simple balance game (*Children's Game #34: Appelsindans* (2022)). When we started filming, two interesting things happened. One is that I filmed mostly with my phone. Although in itself every image was 'true,' little by little I started adjusting my shot, finding the right distance to the players, the best angle, the appropriate height, etc. ... It all happened very quickly and sort of instinctively. The whole thing took at most a couple of hours, with many breaks. The other interesting thing is that when we film with two cameras, whether it is with Rafael or with Julien, it becomes a game of cat and mouse between us. There is a sort of unconscious knowing which field is being covered by the other's camera. A game within the game if you want. I do not remember saying: 'I do this, you do that.' It just happened that Rafa filmed a certain thing, and I filmed something else. Ideally, we will ask to the children to play the game four to five times. That allows us to follow different players and focus on different moments of the action. The repetition is particularly useful when I am filming on my own. After all, games are also about repetition.

Ortega: The first stage is indeed always that you jump into the game. Otherwise, you cannot film it. You need to track the frame because the kids move out of it, and you need to get close to them again. Often, you don't really understand the game, because *they* are playing it. The only way that Francis and I can actually erase ourselves from the cinematic point of view is to somehow become part of the game. That way, the kids do not interact with the camera, and the camera does not become a particular character. This explains why Francis has started using the phone in certain projects. The point of view that he wants to get, you cannot always get with the camera. The collaboration really develops mostly with the children. It is a very interesting kind of pull and let go.

Alÿs: I think that the children accept us because they can see that we take their game very seriously. They appreciate that. Sometimes they can see that we are not fully understanding – we, limited adults – and they will help us grasp the full logic of their actions. They want to give us the best of their skills, what Michael (*Taussig*) indeed calls the "mastery of non-mastery." In all the games we filmed, the children were so much more generous than we expected. Sometimes they even protect us. They for instance make a discreet sign when they see a potential problem or danger rise on the horizon, behind the scene where the game takes place. They can see that we are so absorbed into their play that we are completely unaware of what is happening around us. That happened to me both in the Democratic Republic of the Congo and Iraq.

Ortega: One of the reasons why we both love to do these projects together is that you cannot direct kids. The possibility of a project in which you do not have total control is profoundly attractive. It is fulfilling, since it brings you back to the human humbleness that is necessary to communicate with other people. This is something that I really enjoy. At some point you feel like you have suddenly understood everything, and you realize: this is going to be the perfect shot.

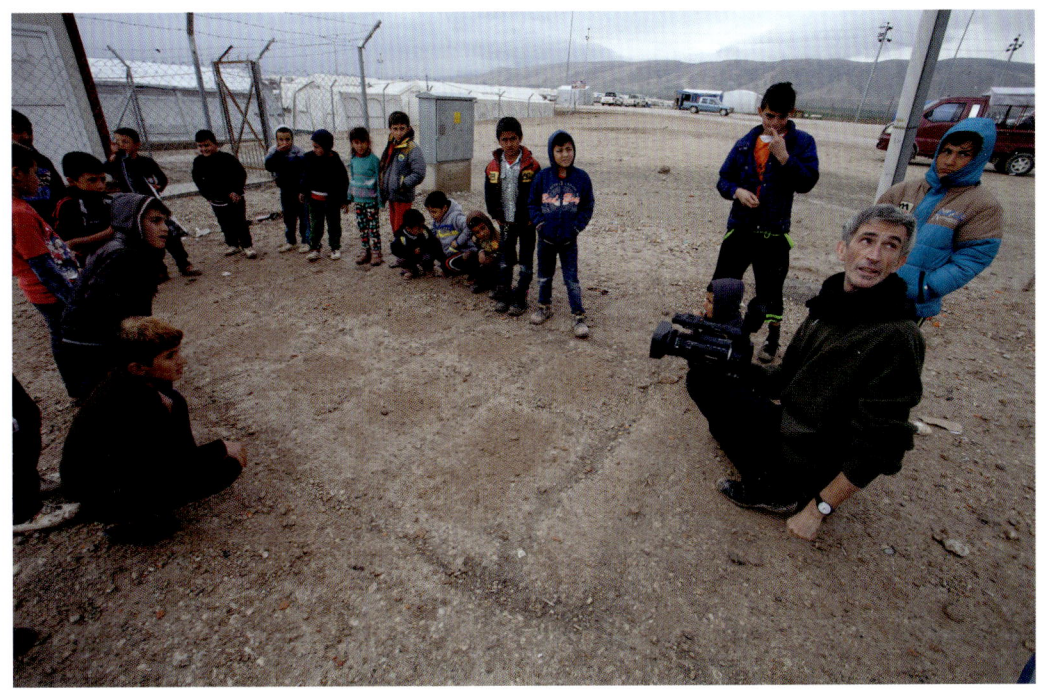

Making of Francis Alÿs, *Children's Game #16: Hopscotch*, Sharya Refugee Camp, Iraq, 2016 (photo by Akam Shex Hadi)

Alÿs: Yes. And when that moment of grace happens, time seems to contract. While you film, you already feel whether this story is going to last four or five or seven minutes, you can sense how long the narrative, the structure, and the development of the game will be.

Ortega: When Francis and I are filming the games, we usually want to just keep on going because we are learning how to film it *while* we are filming it. We are going against the resistance, the time, and the concentration gap that we can find with the children. At some point they will lose interest in the game. There is a very interesting moment when Francis turns around and asks me: 'Do we have it?' It is an incredible moment because we usually have no idea if we have it or not. We just know that we have reached the limits of the children's attention span. From that moment on, we create a backup of the material. Francis keeps a copy, and I keep a copy as well, in case somebody loses the hard drive.

The next step is that Francis and I check the material. I check it more on the technical side, to verify whether it has had exposure, whether it is in focus, whether the sound works, etc. I go over it and randomly pick takes and start watching. And I kind of make a film in my mind while Francis comes up with another film in his editing space.

Alÿs: When editing, the rushes will always be what dictates how to tell the story. You cannot cheat with the material: what you have got is essentially guiding you throughout the editing process. Each *Children's Game* filming comes with a strong sentimental component. It is always a very moving experience, but that is the little story and can be misleading at the moment of editing. You can resist the process of following the rushes and try to fit in every moment and emotion. But you know that, eventually, what does not fit into the narrative will have to be edited out.

Claes: Can we say that the set of rules of the game dictate the form and editing of the video? There are different scopes of production.

Children's Game #29: La roue, for instance, has a larger scope of production than many other videos. How are those choices made?

Ortega: *La roue* is a game that seems very simple. It could have been just one long shot. The guy goes up and comes down, goes up again and comes down again. That's it. But as a filmmaker, you can make the simplest thing hyperbolically complicated. There is no formula for that. In the collaboration with Francis, this shift of the rules is very fascinating. He is open to that shift.

Alÿs: In the case of *La roue* it was the locals – in particular, the 'fixer' – who were really keen on us meeting those kids, *La troupe des acrobates de la mine de Lubumbashi*. They were rehearsing right next to a mine terril, doing all sorts of tricks with big tires with the mine dump as their background. They would also play in some residual dunes right next to the terril. The connection with the Sisyphus myth was obvious.

There are two reflections in response to your question. One is of a more general nature and has to do with the production of my work over the years. If I look back, I went from making personal fictions early on to making a sort of docu-fictions, like the project in Kabul (*Reel-Unreel* (2011)), or the one on the border of Armenia and Turkey (*The Silence of Ani* (2015)). Over the last few years, I have been looking for more of an ethnological documentary approach. The early films of Kiarostami have always been a great guide. I feel very indebted to them. I know it is a bit presumptuous to draw a parallel. But it is funny to think that he started his cinematographic career by making didactical short films with and for children. I might be finishing, or at least completing, mine, with these short didactical videos with children and, hopefully, as well for them.

Anyway, in certain games, the context calls for a more complex reading, a double-layered one if you want. In the case of *La roue*, this had to do with child labor. Directly below the mine terril where we were filming, there was clandestine digging involving child labor. The same exploitative practice was taking place in several villages of Haut-Katanga.

It was impossible to ignore that situation. The game had to somehow address that harsh reality. My response was to make of the children a kind of superheroes who overcome their destiny by subduing the mining dump. They turn the dramatic circumstances around them into a more fictional, ludic world. During the shoot the boys even invented a beautiful song of hope and recovery. It is a debatable decision to give a twist to the documentation of the game, and I have to take it on. I am aware that there are many other ways to address the situation. *Children's Game #15: Espejos* (2013), which was shot in Ciudad Juárez, is somewhat similar. The bits of mirror are like shooting rays that have an almost *Star Wars*-like effect. The game addressed the situation of *narcoviolencia* (drug violence) that deeply affected that community living along the US-Mexico border.

My second reflection comes from having watched the public at the Venice Biennale. I could really feel there were different experiences of watching the games. There were different spans of attention, and so differences in the way the games had been registered. Some of them are a straightforward documentation and, as Rafa said, entirely led by the action. In some other cases, a sort of micro-narrative unfolds throughout the documentation of the game itself. *La roue* and *Espejos* belong to that category. *Children's Game #19: Haram Football* (2017), shot in Mosul, Iraq, belongs to the same category because its historical context was as important as the game itself. You could even say that that game is the direct consequence of a historical moment.

Ortega: Returning to your question about the production of the videos, I want to point out that filmmaking is a *métier*. It is an enormously creative thing and a craft. People do not often realize that a show of thirty games presents an average of one hundred and fifty minutes of film. That is a very long montage. But I do not think that Francis considers himself a filmmaker in any particular way. He considers himself an artist. Filmmaking is just support. The language he uses within the moving image is art. It is contemporary art, not necessarily film or movies. This *métier* of filmmaking probably explains the collaborations with other people. When Francis and I started working together in the nineties, I had already been making films for a good ten years. But I am just one of the collaborators. Félix Blume and Julien Devaux are the other ones.

Alÿs: Indeed, these collaborations are of crucial importance. Julien is an invaluable partner because his approach to filming is quite different from mine. His is more cinematographic, I would say, whereas mine is more punk, as he would say. But we both instinctively feel what images will best tell the story. In a way, our different languages are complementary. Over the years Félix's collaboration in recording and editing the sound grew into a key component of the video documentation of the games. There is so much more emotional power that can be delivered through sound. Both have been extremely generous!

Ortega: Indeed. One of the things we have to point out when we exhibit the *Children's Games* is that you cannot control the sound. You can try to more or less level it but twenty games with five children per game is already one hundred children talking and laughing. When you put one hundred children in a room, you are not going to get a quiet ambience.

IV

Symons: There are two ways of bringing this series to the public. There are the shows, which can indeed have the visual and auditory effect of a chaotic playground, but there is also the website where all of the videos can be quietly looked at, alone and in one's private space. Why did you decide to make the videos available for free, and what kind of spectatorship do you have in mind here?

Alÿs: I do not in any way want to commercialize the films. We do it because we love it. And for the vanity of the arts. Putting them into the domain of the Creative Commons is a direct, clear statement. Also, before I start filming, I always tell all the people involved that they will be able to download and watch the films, that the films will not be commercialized, and that nobody is making money out of this. This makes the relation much healthier. Because it is a question I am often asked, let me add that the children are always paid for their collaboration, or given presents, and so are their parents or family members. The only instance about which I am not sure was in Copenhagen, since the museum (*Copenhagen Contemporary*) was in charge of the production. On some occasions donations were made to the local school or youth club.

Ortega: The question of social media is interesting here. When you put something in the domain of the Creative Commons, people make it theirs. This is very interesting for me because it puts me into contact with a lot of people. I meet all kinds of people who work with children or, for instance, visit refugee camps to help children as part of NGO work. Some of these people have used the *Children's Games* as a trigger to talk to children in particular situations. A friend of mine works as a psychiatric researcher and uses the *Children's Games* with some of the patients to talk about their memories of childhood. The series has become something completely and gloriously uncontrollable. In some way, social media is part of the spirit of the project. The series is about making visible. We see something that is not often seen. We want to witness and share these things.

Alÿs: Social media is the reality of our times. When I am on the subway, lots of people are watching 'reels' on their phone. I often find myself peeping over their shoulders to see what they're watching. What is it that captures people's imagination and fantasy, and where do we filmmakers and artists stand in the infinite proliferation of images of our times? We are at the dawn of a new era. I feel like a dinosaur, yet I want to be part of that conversation. Social media is a revolutionary platform. Some kids film a dog-and-cat fight in their backyard. It then goes viral and within a week has reached millions of viewers. How can we compete with that?

Ortega: We wake up every morning saying: 'Who needs another video?'

Alÿs: Absolutely. Nowadays, to show, to present something is a complete blind date. You do not know how people are going to react. There are so many new parameters, not just about the content, but also about authorship and the context, even about the language. But I must say that the response in Venice came as a great surprise. The installation was complete madness because we had changed the project a few months earlier and the timing was extremely tight. The last game had been shot six weeks before the opening, and most games were filmed during the pandemic. Some videos, like *Children's Game #30: Imbu* (2021), were still being edited while we were installing. Still, we managed to make contact with the audience in Venice. Maybe this was due to certain external factors, for instance, our coming out of the pandemic lockdowns, the sudden realization that watching children playing on the street is becoming a scene of the past, the then recent entry of Russian troops into Ukraine ... Who knows. But something happened. Lots of people were very moved while visiting the pavilion. Some cried, some laughed, there were lots of emotions flying in the air, and the need of the visitors to watch convivial events together. François Truffaut once said that cinematic success is not always the result of good brainwork but can also just be an accidental coincidence of our own preoccupations and the public's.

Claes: The *Children's Games* contain documentary shots but never present a mere *couleur locale*. There is always a certain distance. Does this mean that you already have an interpretation in mind while filming? And is this interpretation part of the artistic process?

Alÿs: I am sure I often arrive at the filming location with my *petites histoires* in mind. However, the game's action will quickly take over. Even my own understanding and interpretation of the game will evolve during the making. In a sense, everyone finds something different in them, or recognizes something different; games are very rich in meanings and generous in potential readings. It is not for me to interfere with that process. Not to mention that I have chosen to produce images because of my limits with speech. I like to keep their reading open.

When I am on location behind the camera, I am essentially trying to coincide with the moment. And, when editing, to stay true to my experience of that moment. This does not necessarily mean to simply reproduce the scene as it happened. It's about choosing and assembling images that will recreate for someone else the emotional bubble you were in. To achieve that, one has to sometimes fictionalize details.

Ortega: This emotional sphere, and staying true to it, is something that really cannot be explained. For instance, some people draw the camera to them. In those cases, you know perfectly well that taking your camera away from them will mean that they are not going to exist in the film. As a filmmaker, you have an intuition that the camera has to be drawn to these particular people at that specific moment. I have told Francis a thousand times about one of the rules that stuck with me when I was starting film school: 'If you did not film it, you cannot edit it.' You cannot try to go there later if you have initially missed it. Francis and I can be intuitive with certain things.

Symons: Did this emotional sphere change in any way since you started the series almost twenty-five years ago? I am thinking of, amongst other things, the personal use of cameras and the self-awareness that this brings. Do you have the feeling that the young people you are filming have become less spontaneous and, perhaps, are losing the ability to be immersed in play?

Alÿs: Regardless of the presence of a camera, the playing always ends up taking over. I am thinking of *Children's Game #34: Appelsindans.* During the first couple of games, they were laughing and there was a lot of …

Ortega: … fooling around!

Alÿs: Yes. The same thing tends to happen on many occasions. In the first couple of games the kids are joking and laughing a lot. By the third go, they are becoming more competitive, and by the fifth it'll be more about skills and who takes the lead. This brings me to another aspect: no matter how much we try to give a 'horizontal' representation of the game – including all the players both in the filming and its editing – there are inevitably some children who end up taking a more protagonistic role. They will become the characters that will run the game. But we always make sure that all participants appear.

Ortega: I do notice a change in the emotional sphere of a game. There used to be moments when you were filming a child and the child had no idea that he was being filmed. Perhaps nobody had ever filmed him before. But now, at least the kids we filmed in *Children's Game #34: Appelsindans* have been filmed since they were born. I am not saying that they are image conscious already, but they are conscious that the camera is there and that it is registering something that they are doing. There is a much shorter margin these days: if the game does not take over immediately, Francis and I cannot make a video. If they do not get into the game, they start to realize we are filming, and they might no longer want to be filmed. Sometimes we have to interrupt the game. We might ask them to have a biscuit and explain that everything is going fine. Or we might put them in a circle and ask them how they are feeling, invite them to get their hands up or loosen up. Sometimes we might do something funny or try to re-engage them.

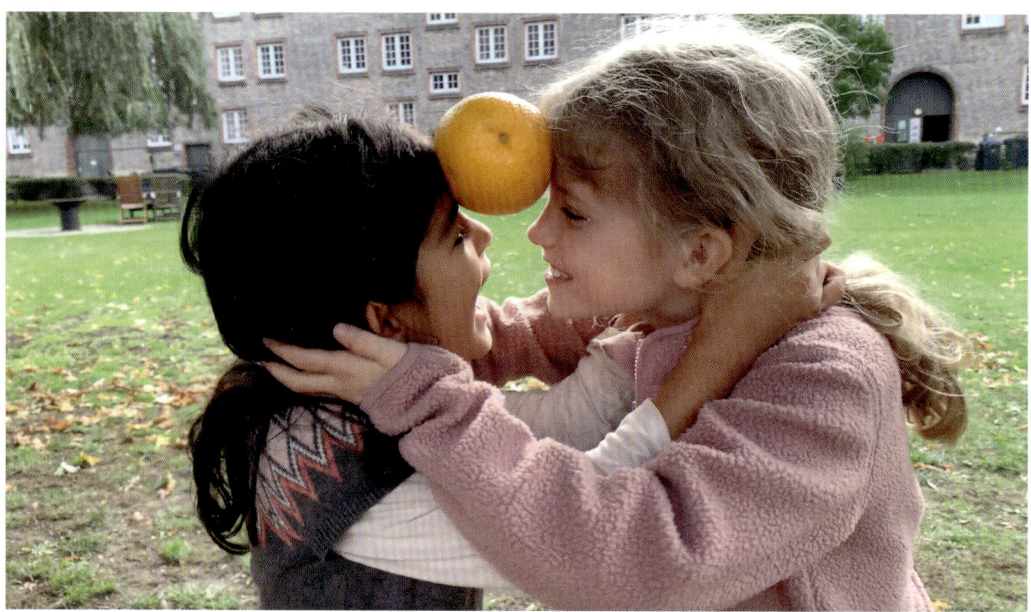

Francis Alÿs, *Children's Game #34: Appelsindans*, Copenhagen, Denmark, 2022 (still)

Alÿs: Let me tell you what happened when we presented *Children's Game #29: La roue* in Lubumbashi to the community where the games were filmed. The video is fairly long, eight and a half minutes, but after four-and-a-half minutes the children who played in the video stood up and started a choreographed cheering in which they were raising their arms, chanting, and dancing. They did this three or four times over the course of the screening. They wanted to interact directly with the moving image projected behind them. Interestingly, when they were doing this, they were looking at the public, and no longer at the images …

Whenever possible, I try to present the films where they have been produced. It was possible in Afghanistan, thanks to my friend and collaborator Ajmal Maiwandi. In Iraq, too, it was possible to present *Sandlines, The Story of History* (2018–2020), a feature film enacted by the children of a small mountain village near Mosul. But we could only show them the first cut, not the film's final version. To return the story to the community can change things. In Iraq, for example, the screening took place before the second and final shoot. Initially, the girls of the village had not been allowed to participate, but after seeing the first cut, they really wanted to participate. This time their parents allowed them to. Their entry opened up the story and made me completely change the script. Eventually, it allowed us to find a way out of the story, and it's the girls who had the last word.

It is never easy to show your own work but the toughest test is when you show it to the people you filmed. It's the moment you are most vulnerable and … naked. It is also the moment where you instantly see all the mistakes you made in the editing. The viewers might not even notice it, but just their breathing will tell you when a scene is three seconds too long, or five seconds too short, or simply not necessary. The critical reading that the participants of the film offer is unique. Just sitting with them and watching the video together makes you instantly step out of the fantasy you had created in your editing room.

Presenting the film to the people who performed it is also a very humbling experience. You wish you could have done better. Almost always. Only in a few rare cases, the opposite occurs. You realize how fortunate you were to capture a moment that will not repeat itself. Not for them, not for you. As an artist, as an author, as a filmmaker, this is what keeps you going. Those moments of grace when you coincide with a collective reality. They are what keeps you in the game.

Notes

1. Michael Taussig (2020). *Mastery of Non-Mastery in the Age of Meltdown.* Chicago: University of Chicago Press.

Children's Games. A Reflection on the Work of Francis Alÿs

Tim Ingold*

I

"It keeps my 3-year-old boy entertained for ages." These words were posted by a satisfied customer in an anonymous review of the *Hungry Hippos Game*, one of hundreds of children's games which I picked out, more or less at random, from an online catalogue. The game comes packed in an attractive cardboard box, the contents of which include a game base, four plastic hippo heads, four tails which work as levers, twenty marbles, and an instruction booklet. Up to four players compete to project the marbles, by means of the levers, into the hippos' open mouths. The winner's hippo gobbles the most marbles.

In the commercial world of children's entertainment, the game is a commodity and game-playing a variety of consumption. Parents in a consumer-oriented society, in which time at home is to be used up, face a constant struggle to keep their offspring occupied. Children need to have something to do, lest they grow bored and listless. Yet all consumption depletes the stock with which it begins. It starts with a full supply and ends when it runs out. The question is: how long can you string it out? Give the child a game to play, and it is soon finished. What then? They may repeat it, again and again, but every replay brings diminishing returns of gratification and a growing impatience for something new, driving the frustrated parent back to the catalogue.

* Tim Ingold is Emeritus Professor of Social Anthropology at the University of Aberdeen, and a Fellow of the British Academy and the Royal Society of Edinburgh.

The market for children's games depends, of course, on making sure that children soon get bored with them, and games are designed with this tedium in mind. Initially stacked high on the shelves of toyshops or online distribution centers, most will end up abandoned in the attic or find their way to a recycling depot or charity shop. Sandwiched between distribution and abandonment or between one stack and another, gaming pieces enjoy only a brief outing in the hands of the children for whom they are intended. The review of *Hungry Hippos* was posted on May 18, 2018. Now that I write this, in March 2023, the little boy it entertained 'for ages' will be a lad of around 8 years. He will surely have long since tired of projecting marbles into the hippos' mouths. Most probably, he has forsaken the cartoonish menagerie of plastic hippopotami to play out equally contrived but more exciting adventures on screen.

II

Could it be otherwise? Picture an alternative reality, in which our eight-year-old is from a poor family that cannot afford to be constantly buying game sets for the children, let alone computers with expensive accessories for them to play on. For this boy the home offers little comfort, and life is lived predominantly beyond its walls. He could be one from the huddle of lads, ranging in age from around seven to fourteen, whom Francis Alÿs filmed in Amman, Jordan's capital city (*Children's Game #8: Marbles* (2010)). They are engrossed in a game of marbles, played on a patch of wasteland adjoining a busy road and a railway track. The boys have made a small round hole in the dirt. Each player, using his thumb and index finger, attempts to flick his marble to reach the hole in as few steps as possible, while knocking away the marbles of his opponents. He can keep any marble he knocks out. The player who collects the most marbles wins. Yet winning is only a passing matter

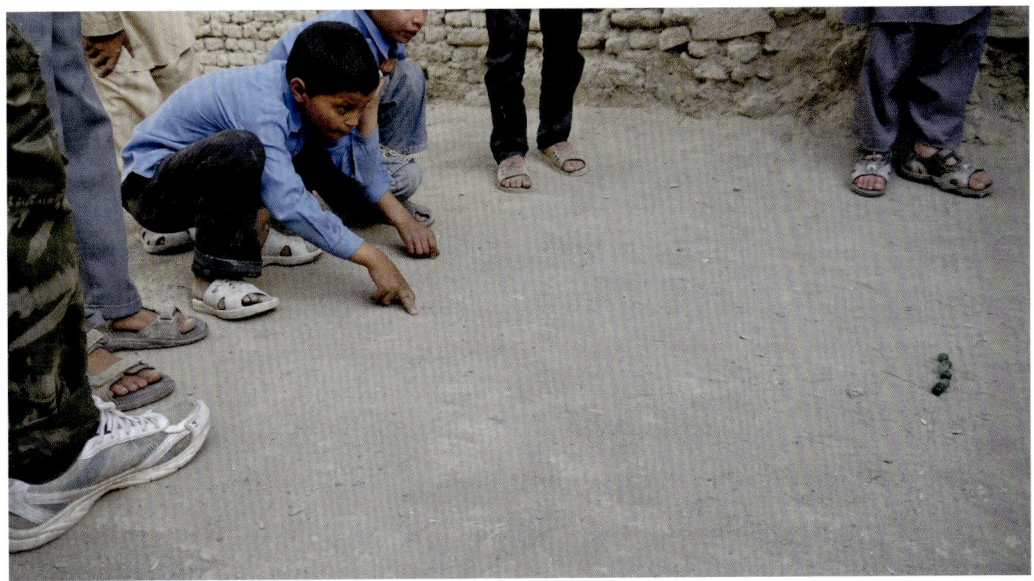

Making of Francis Alÿs, *Children's Game #8: Marbles*, Amman, Jordan, 2010 (photo by the artist)

since it invariably heralds the start of another round. The game itself carries on indefinitely or until the players drift off.

In purely formal terms, this game shares many features with *Hungry Hippos*: both games are played with marbles; in both, players project the marbles into an aperture, and in both the winner is the one with the most. Beyond the formal resemblance, however, the game of marbles we see being played here is everything that *Hungry Hippos* is not. We could start with the fact that it is played in the open air. There is a constant roar of traffic in the background, while a call to prayer, broadcast from loudspeakers, echoes over the rooftops of apartment blocks. Somewhere far off, what sounds like an ice-cream van plays its tune. The game is staged, then, not in a boxed-up, fantasy setting – such as between the covers of a storybook, inside the home, and under the supervision of an adult – but in the familiar haunt of a real-world cityscape, in a no-man's-land in between the spaces of its architectural and transport infrastructure, where kids can meet on their own terms.

The hole in the dirt brings this world to a focus. Observe the cluster of marbles in the hole, and you will see, reflected in their surfaces, not just the boys' faces but the sunlight, the sky, the buildings, everything. As in a vortex, the hole is formed as an eye around which the game swirls, drawing players and onlookers alike into its orbit for as long as it turns. Playing the game is thus a way of place-making. It makes a place in the wasteland, where there was none before. Where *Hungry Hippos*, enclosed within its storybook bubble, offers a brief escape into fantasy, the game played here brings everyone down to earth – literally, since you must crouch down to flick the marbles and scoop the dirt to recover them. Moreover, unlike pulling the levers of the hippos' tails, in which one pull is as good as another and the outcome largely up to chance, the finger-flick calls for consummate skill and precision, and successful execution draws admiration from bystanders.

III

The manual dexterity of these young marble-players is indeed astonishing. Yet it is not unusual. Many of the children's games from around the world, which Alÿs has caught on camera, celebrate the dexterity demonstrated by the players: the youth who skims stones far over the waters of a bay in Tangier, Morocco (*Children's Game #2: Ricochets* (2007)); the pair of girls playing knucklebones in Kathmandu, Nepal, who can toss a pile of pebbles only to catch them on the back of the same hand (*Children's Game #18: Knucklebones* (2017)); the three girls who meet on a rooftop in Hong Kong to practice their virtuoso routines of rope-skipping (*Children's Game #22: Jump Rope* (2020)). Unlike the game-in-a-box, the parameters of which are predetermined, marbles, stones, pebbles, and ropes do not come with instructions attached. They do not tell the player what to do with them. Only as they are brought into play do they come into their own.

The freedom they afford is not therefore to be found in the choice of moves or in the indeterminacy of their outcomes, but in the movement itself and in its attunement to things and the ways they want to go. That's where the skill lies. It is evident from the faces of the young players that skilled performance calls for great concentration. Equally evident, though, is the satisfaction it brings. It is a satisfaction, however, that could not be more different from the immediate gratification afforded by a game like *Hungry Hippos*. It comes not from the fulfillment of a need or desire, but from discovering that you can do things beyond what you had previously imagined possible. Fulfillment brings closure, but discovery opens a path to growth. Skill is grown, or produced, in the activity, not used up or consumed. There is no limit to its perfection.

Moreover, it is produced not individually but mutually. The little boy reported by his parent to have been entertained for ages by *Hungry*

Hippos might not have played alone, since up to four can join the game. But whatever gratification it brings accrues to each player as an individual. Not so, however, for skilled marble-flickers, stone-skimmers, knucklebones-throwers, and rope-skippers, who entertain themselves in the far more fundamental and literal sense – from the Latin *inter*, 'between', plus *tenere*, 'to hold' – of *holding on to one another*, in relations of mutual support. Entertainment, here, is a mode not of individual consumption, confined to the home, but of collective production, in the open space of the commons. It is the way in which, in a collective, everyone raises each other up.

IV

Such entertainment, in turn, can be a source of joy. In another of Alÿs's films, of children from Engelberg, Switzerland, playing in the snow, their sheer joyfulness has to be seen to be believed (*Children's Game #33: Schneespiele* (2022)). The children cannot contain their delight, and it bursts out, not just in the radiance of their facial expressions but in their screams of surprise and pleasure. Their play is entirely improvised. It has no rules and requires no apparatus apart from warm clothing. One moment they are hurling snowballs at each other, the next moment sliding down a slippery slope – first singly, then altogether in a train – and finally teaming up to roll the snow into a hulk that will perhaps become the body of a snowman. The fluidity of their collaboration is extraordinary.

Can there be joy, then, only in the gathering of many lives, in the sympathetic union of their collective endeavor? Does it call for a veritable chorus of feet, hands, faces, and voices – as in the boys' game of stacking hands, which Alÿs filmed in Nerkzlia, Iraq (*Children's Game #21: Hand Stack* (2019)), or in the girls' game of Nzango, popular in the Democratic Republic of the Congo, with its lightning-fast coordination of rapid foot movements (*Children's Game #28: Nzango* (2021))? In short, can anyone, be they child or grown-up, find joy in solitude?

In the city of Hong Kong, a little girl cruises joyously along streets and pavements (*Children's Game #23: Step on a Crack* (2020)). Perhaps she is on her way home from school. Purposefully hopping over every crack in the pavement and every painted line of a street crossing, she escapes the grid that holds everyone else in its grip. It is as though she were floating like a sprite, visible to others only as a will-o'-the-wisp. People turn to stare, alerted by her passing, but see nothing. She has become an aerial being. So, too, has the little boy filmed in Balkh, Afghanistan, who is flying a kite (*Children's Game #10: Papalote* (2011)). Manipulating the string in deft, rapid movements, he plays the kite like a musical instrument. His body may be on the ground, but the music of his spirit soars with the wind. Both street-hopping and kite-flying seem to proclaim the triumph of grace over gravity, of lines of flight over the weight of oppression. They undoubtedly bring joy. And yet it seems a solitary joy, far from the collective exuberance of the chorus.

V

Yet the solitude of the street-hopper or the kite-flyer is quite unlike the loneliness of the parent, stuck at home, struggling to keep their child entertained, or even of the anonymous city dweller in a crowd. The solitary are never alone since, unlike the lonely, they are not shut off from their surroundings so much as opened to them, in the heightened perceptual awareness of being in the midst of things. And their joy comes from this awareness. It is not an inward pleasure, registered in isolation. Nor can it be produced to order as the effect of any determinate set of causes. It cannot, in other words, be manufactured for consumption or bought and sold over the counter. You cannot put joy in a box, for its very nature is spontaneity and excess. Trying to catch it is as futile as attempting to catch the wind in a jar. Like the wind, as the kite-flyer will tell you, you cannot touch joy but you can feel it, by the way it wraps around your body and buoys it up as if you were floating in the air.

Nothing exemplifies this better than the game of *Imbu*, filmed in Tabacongo, Democratic Republic of the Congo (*Children's Game #30: Imbu* (2021)). A bunch of young boys are clustered together with their faces upturned, hands cupping their lips, as they chant in sustained, overlapping monotones, their voices lifting up over one another in an eerie but joyful chorus. The performance is a mystery until you see the swarm of mosquitoes rising in a column above their heads. To the mosquitoes the sound is irresistible, and by stretching their arms towards the heavens and clapping their hands, players try to swat as many as they can. In this extraordinary concert, the cluster of bodies on the ground is transformed into a swirl of voices in the air, each seeking its insect partner, only to lure the latter to its death. Here, joy is genuinely airborne until it falls to earth. This has its parallel, perhaps, among the children of Salto Acha, Venezuela, who love to catch grasshoppers in the undergrowth. Ripping off their hind legs while leaving the wings intact, the children fly them like miniature helicopters until they drop (*Children's Game #9: Saltamontes* (2011)).

Not much fun, then, for the insects. But what of the larger animals accustomed to the spaces of human domesticity? Do they, too, feel the joy of being alive, as children do? Whereas grown-up humans are mainly conspicuous by their absence from Alÿs's films of children's games, domestic animals often figure in them, mostly however as nonchalant bystanders, casting a benevolent eye on the proceedings without being tempted to intervene, as grown-up humans might. A rumbustious game of tag among the children of Malinalco, Mexico, is quietly observed by a horse and a pig, though a dog does its best to join in. In Tabacongo, a hen scuttles through the middle of a game of marbles, amidst much hilarity.

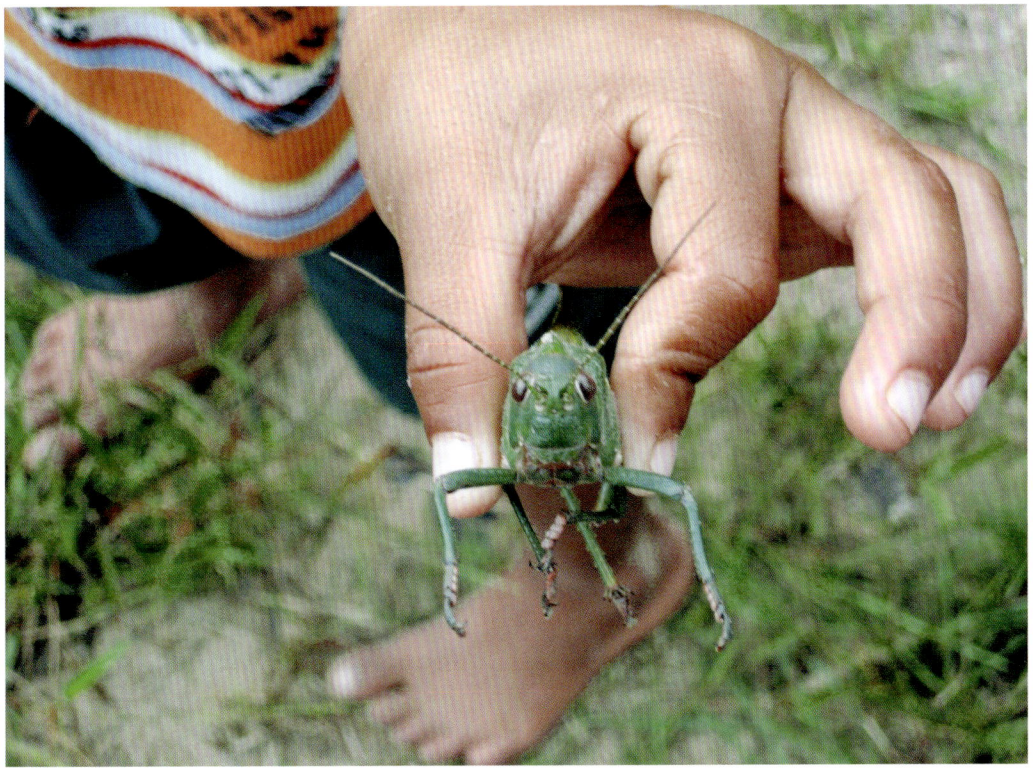

Francis Alÿs, *Children's Game #9: Saltamontes*, Salto Acha, Venezuela, 2011 (still)

And in Nerkzlia, Iraq, a goat finds itself unwittingly co-opted into a game of leapfrog, and bleats loudly: is it in protest or because it resents being left behind? Two snails, raced by children in Pajottenland, Belgium, strike a photo finish but appear supremely uninterested until a shower of rain brings them relief and sends the children racing for cover (*Children's Game #25: Contagio* (2021), *Children's Game #27: Rubi* (2021), *Children's Game #20: Leap Frog* (2018), *Children's Game #31: Slakken* (2021)).

VI

Outside affluent countries of the Global North such as Belgium and Switzerland, however, or beyond a great megalopolis like Hong Kong with its towering skyscrapers, the one virtual constant of these children's games is that they are played in landscapes of ruination. In Lubumbashi, Democratic Republic of the Congo, children roll tires, and themselves inside them, down the slopes of an immense, toxic slag heap rising in the shadow of a cobalt mine. In Ciudad Juárez, Mexico, they practice a shootout amidst the remains of half-built homes in a patch of desolate grassland, firing the sun's rays using fragments of a broken mirror. In Sharya Refugee Camp, Iraq, they play hopscotch on waste ground behind which looms a forest of tents, now their only homes. And in Mosul they play football on the street – only without a ball – against a background of burned-out vehicles and shelled buildings, their walls and turrets askew, where only two years earlier, in 2015, an Islamic State firing squad had publicly executed thirteen teenagers merely for the 'crime' of having watched a match on television (*Children's Game #29: La roue* (2021), *Children's Game #15: Espejos* (2013), *Children's Game #16: Hopscotch* (2016), *Children's Game #19: Haram Football* (2017)).

Neither children nor animals bear any responsibility for this mess. It is entirely the responsibility of grown men who have sought to use the raw power and technological means of mass destruction at their disposal to enrich themselves and enforce their rule upon the powerless, including women and children, and of course animals. Power, however, not only kills people and poisons their environments; it also drains the powerful of their own vitality. There can be no enjoyment in the exercise of oppression. And yet, even the powerful were children once. They might have raced and skipped, laughed and clapped their hands in delight, as children do. But look at them now! Po-faced and glum, their glazed eyes stare out in bitter disdain for all they survey.

What has happened? Is it inevitable that today's joyous children will become the killjoys of tomorrow? Must each generation, as it matures, turn upon its past, to become the oppressors of the next? Is the grace of childhood destined to be crushed, every time, by the weight of adult domination? Can there really be no joy save in the midst of suffering? To argue that the only true joy is to be found in the freedom of the oppressed, as some have done, is to reproduce the conditions of subjugation, not to extinguish them. If generations could but learn to work together in co-producing the future, in a spirit of companionship rather than confrontation, how much more enjoyable, and indeed more entertaining, our lives could be!

Francis Alÿs. Children's Games

Karen Lang*

> *Hope is invented every day.*
> —James Baldwin (1970)

I

"But if I were to make what you call 'a more complete story,' a feature film, I would not start at the beginning or the end," mused Francis Alÿs in an early interview. "I would need to work from some middle, because the middle point, the in-between, is the space where I function best."[1] In Alÿs's recent film *Sandlines, the Story of History* (2018–2020), the children of a mountain village near Mosul recreate a century of Iraqi history from some point between official history and themselves. Yet we need not have waited to see that Alÿs's creations arise from "the middle point, the in-between." Like a cat's cradle, his working notes for the action *The Logic of Ñandū* (2005) chart a course through the in-between, ending in "the shadow". This shadow might also be the shadow cast by "doubting," the first term (the first play) in this scheme, the point from which the action unfurls. Will we end up where we began? The artist never knows himself. It's up to the play of the action, and the play of the action transpires in the action itself.

Indeed, play is the pivot of Alÿs's artistic practice. In his book *Homo Ludens*, written in the middle of the Nazi threat in the mid-1930s, Dutch historian Johan Huizinga offers the following definition of play:

* Karen Lang is Professor of Art History and Fellow of the Royal Society of Arts.

Summing up the formal characteristics of play we might call it a free activity standing quite consciously outside "ordinary" life as being "not serious", but at the same time absorbing the player intensely and utterly. It is an activity connected with no material interest, and no profit can be gained by it. It proceeds within its own proper boundaries of time and space according to fixed rules and in an orderly manner.[2]

French sociologist Roger Caillois has criticized Huizinga's exclusion from the definition of play games of chance played for money, noting the abundance of gambling houses, casinos, racetracks, and lotteries in societies of the West.[3] Yet one could argue that games of chance played for money, like the actual war games we can envision Huizinga following on the radio, are neither entirely voluntary or free, since the rules of these games are set by persons or structures other than the participants (or listeners). For Huizinga and Alÿs, play stands outside 'ordinary' life, is voluntary and free, is something we create even as we submit to it. Entering the magic circle of play, the players set the rules but play proceeds of itself: play occurs in the intermediate playground between the players and play itself.

In the play of the action, all the elements of Alÿs's artistic practice – art and storytelling, poetics and politics, hope and freedom – appear between the lines. Curator Russell Ferguson asks in this same early interview: "Either the story or the image can work in your mind, or your collaborator's mind, or the viewer's mind, and generate some other event or image." To which Alÿs rejoins: "Yes, it is always kind of bouncing or richocheting."[4] Whether playing or playing up, story and image have a life of their own. The creator Alÿs sets the play in motion and follows where it leads.

"In the beginning of art," Alÿs has said, "there is this spacing that isn't a space, a void between two things in which art becomes possible, and it must be marked each time, for it is what art 'is', a mere 'nothing' that isn't nothing, since it happens."[5] If art emerges in "a void between two things," then art is nothing more but also nothing less than the occasion of this emergence. In fact, all the elements of Alÿs's artistic practice are nothing more and nothing less than the occasion of this emergence. "If the story is good enough," he continues, "it will get back to you or achieve its shape by itself. If it isn't, then it's better for it to die away."[6]

Alÿs's creations open new spaces and remind us of hidden ones. They hinge on the existence and possibility of invention. Wherever one happens to be, come what may. Notice how the previous sentence, "Wherever one happens to be, come what may", marks out a space or void for invention. What do I mean? When I write "Wherever one happens to be, come what may" the comma is a hinge: the comma opens a space or void for invention. You, the reader, can travel through my sentence from left to right or right to left of the comma without any loss in meaning. And not only that. My sentence invites you to linger at the comma, to swing left or right, right or left, in the void thus invented. The comma is, we might say, an invitation to linger. It is also an enticement to discover – in a moment, in a flash – what arises, for you, in the space between wherever we happen to be and come what may. It is in just this way that the creations of Francis Alÿs travel into us and work upon us: they open a void in which precious elements of human life might be encountered or remembered.

Alÿs's creations show us that art and storytelling, poetics and politics, hope and freedom are invented every day, between the lines, even in situations pitted against human possibility. For James Baldwin, an American writer known for his anti-racist humanism, a long history of racial injustice against the 'American Negro' revealed that hope for survival, hope for change, hope for justice, is invented every day. Alÿs invents by conjuring or capturing actions in which the elements of his art can appear. He mentions to Russell Ferguson that all his projects "try to be part of a single narrative."[7] I would say that single narrative is this: human life exists between the lines of societal structures and strictures, and where there is human life, there is hope.

II

Walking features in Alÿs's artistic practice from the beginning. Having relocated to Mexico City in the wake of the devastating earthquake of 1985, he set out from his studio in the historic center and walked the streets. He stuffed pillows in broken windows. Poetic and political, this action emerged from and filled a gap. Yet there is more here than meets the eye. This action brings the causes of ruination into focus, not only the earthquake but also the latent power structures of the built environment. In a later action titled *Fairy Tales*, Alÿs walked through a wooded park in Stockholm as a loose thread on his sweater unravelled, leaving a trail behind him. In 1995, for the São Paolo Biennale, he walked and dripped a leaking can of blue paint away from the gallery and back, hanging the empty paint can on the wall inside the gallery.

In 2004, Alÿs re-enacted the earlier performance in São Paolo by walking and dripping a line of green paint along the portion of the 'green line' that runs through the municipality of Jerusalem. The 'green line' is "the internationally recognized eastern border of Israel, which it overran in June 1967."[8] Eyal Weizman tells us that the 'green line,' first drawn as a ceasefire line in 1948, "tore apart" Arab and Jewish communities "that had a complicated, shared, urban life."[9] Alÿs's action responds implicitly to this frayed history. *The Green Line* (2004) is motivated by two inter-related axioms, which he has called 'the paradox of praxis': "Sometimes doing something poetic can become political, and sometimes doing something political can become poetic." *The Green Line* (2004) pivots on the comma in between the two axioms: like the comma, the axioms swing both ways and do not settle. Instead of fixing the outcome, *The Green Line* (2004) opens a void through which poetics may encounter politics and vice versa. Shortly thereafter, Alÿs presented a filmed documentation of the walk to a number of people who were invited "to react spontaneously to the action and the circumstances within which it was performed."[10] The action unspools further "when it is constituted in the viewer."[11]

In *Paradox of Praxis #5* (2013), Alÿs kicked a soccerball-sized ball of fire through the dusky streets of Ciudad Juárez, a populous Mexican city on the Rio Grande. The filmed documentation locates the viewer inside the cat's cradle of two axioms which weave and unwind as the action progresses: "Sometimes we dream as we live, sometimes we live as we dream." While it is clear the action takes place in the streets of a real city, the overall mood is redolent of fairy tales. A spell is cast but not entirely. Art makes its appearance between the lines of the mundane, and this work gathers power from its unsettled location between reality and dream.

Alÿs is interested in more than artistic interventions as occurrences in the real world. He is inspired by the way these actions "can also travel as an anecdote or fable,"[12] taking on new life in new contexts. The latter point is crucial. To be fruitful, Alÿs's creations must have the capacity to be invented or reinvented everyday – not only to emerge, but to travel, and in travelling, to change. Once again we hit on the point that these creations must have a life of their own.

Perhaps this is why Alÿs prefers to be called a creator rather than an artist. In our time, the word 'artist' (for which read 'successful artist') conjures an image of the lone maker who is a savvy player of the global art-world game. (Never mind if this successful artist has a raft of assistants, the image of the lone maker holds because hierarchy is implied in the bargain.) The word 'creator,' on the other hand, still has a whiff of art for art's sake about it, of making above all else, perhaps together with others. Alÿs is known for working collaboratively (Cuauhtémoc Medina, Rafael Ortega, Félix Blume, and Julien Devaux are long-term collaborators). His artistic process continues to involve local participants on site. Yet the role of the viewer is crucial, too.

German philosopher Hans-Georg Gadamer reminds us that "any creation that we call a work of art [...] demands to be constructed by the viewer to whom it is presented." As if foretelling Alÿs's own words about the void that makes art possible, Gadamer wrote that the work of art "is not simply what it is, but rather something that it is not." The work of art, he continues, "is not something we can simply use for a particular purpose, nor a material thing from which we might fabricate some other thing. On the contrary, it is something that only manifests and displays itself when it is constituted in the viewer."[13] It is worthwhile noting that Gadamer is not saying that the work of art is constituted according to the viewer's subjectivity. (He is not saying that the work of art is whatever we may think or say about it.) Instead, his point is ethical: the subject of the work of art is the work of art itself, not the subjectivity of the viewer. In the encounter between the work of art and the viewer the work of art is "constituted in the viewer," and it is this take-up of the work inside ourselves which enables us to see the world according to the perspective of the work of art, rather than our own. It is in this way that the work of art reveals the world to us as if we are seeing it for the first time.

III

All the elements of Alÿs's artistic practice emerge in *Children's Games* (1999–ongoing). Viewing this series of some thirty short films shot mainly in the Global South, it is striking to discover similarities in play around the world. The note of common humanity is less resonant, however, than the particularity of each child, each location, each rendering of the game. Indeed, we are a long way from the universal sense of humanity espoused in *The Family of Man*, the acclaimed exhibition of photographs curated by Edward Steichen for the Museum of Modern Art, New York, at the height of the Cold War in 1955.[14] Rather than universal humanity at play, it is the commonality of play which strikes us in *Children's Games*. We recognize that play is particular and adaptable, that rituals of play emerge between the strictures of existence and irrepressible forces of imagination. If there is a guiding thread in the series *Children's Games*, it is that rituals of play are invented every day, even in situations pitted against human possibility.[15]

Alÿs has recently remarked upon the inspiration of Pieter Bruegel's *Children's Games*, painted in 1560, which he first saw as a child in Belgium.[16] The inventory of games and chaos of the playground recall his own series of short films. In all these works, the impulse to inventory collides with the freedom of play. While games might be inventoried according to type or shared characteristics, play, as Huizinga said, "is not susceptible to exact definition either logically, biologically, or aesthetically. Child and animal play because they enjoy playing, and therein precisely lies their freedom."[17] Across the distances of time and genre, Bruegel and Alÿs capture the freedom of play for its own sake. Just as these works show the characteristics of play – its secludedness, disinterestedness, limitedness, tension – so they reveal what it means to be captivated by play, to be in the hands of a force which is so freeing. "For play has its own essence, independent of the consciousness of those who play,"[18] Gadamer insisted. And so it is in these works: play rolls the dice.

Art, play, playfulness, gesture – each emerges in a middle ground or void in-between. By drawing a circle on the ground, children mark out a time and space for playfulness. By pushing a tire or ball away at the end of the game, they signal that special time and place has come to end. Philosophers tell us that at the heart of play is a disposition or tendency called playfulness: "a way of being, a way of doing – a mode of existence

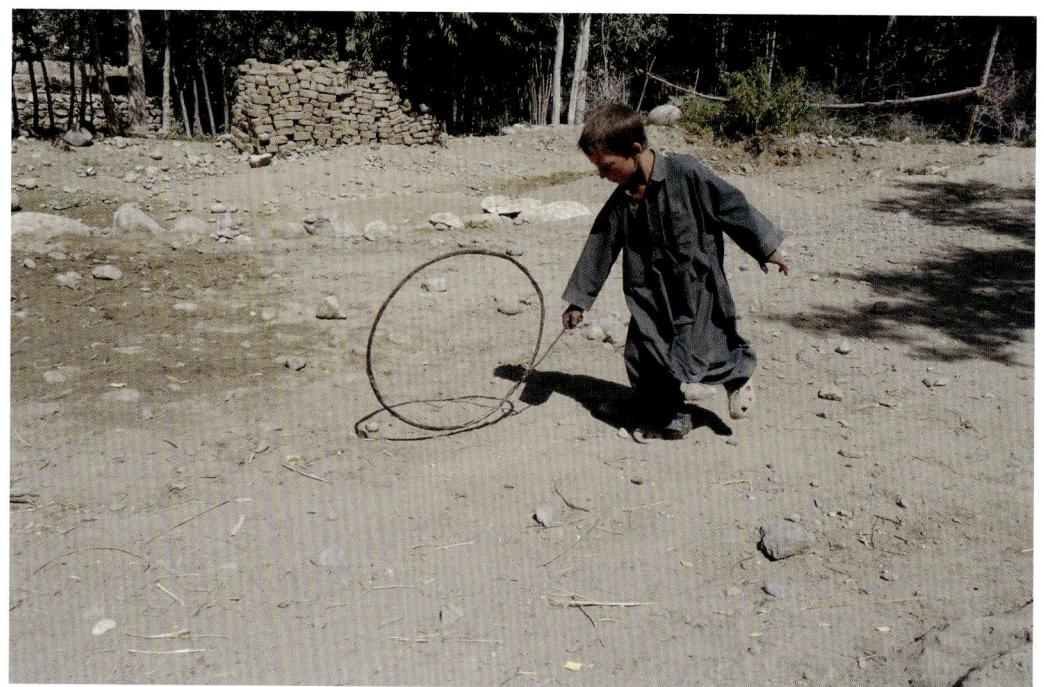

Making of Francis Alÿs, *Children's Game #7: Stick and Wheels*, Bamiyan, Afghanistan, 2010 (photo by the artist)

that we bring into being in a situation […] that is a precondition for play to emerge."[19] Playfulness is neither deterministic nor calculable, but ontological, "a way of being, a way of doing," which takes place in a time and space apart from ordinary life.[20] When we play, we reorient ourselves toward the greatest sense of the world, beyond what the eye has seen or the mind has known. When we are absorbed utterly in play, we touch this world beyond with our senses. As Gadamer said, "What a gesture expresses is 'there' in the gesture itself. A gesture is something wholly corporeal and wholly spiritual at one and the same time."[21]

The children of the Yazidi community, who play hopscotch on the fringes of the Sharya Refugee Camp in Iraq in *Children's Game #16: Hopscotch* (2016), reinvent the gestures of their ancestors for whom to hop between earth and heaven was to be reborn. Three boys from Tangier, Morocco, skim stones over the sea in *Children's Game #2: Ricochets* (2007). Although the gesture is futile, since the sea will always outrun the stone, these boys play to the tilt nonetheless: one boy provides the stones, one skims them over the sea, one observes and encourages. Watching the film, we enter the imaginative order of the game, become rhythm to its rhythm, like the boy hurling the stone becomes one with the changing pattern of the waves, the better to reach further across the sea with his stone. In *Children's Game #19: Haram Football* (2017), the game is imaginary but the stakes are real and dangerous. In a street surrounded by ruins in Mosul, Iraq, young people re-enact for the camera a game of 'forbidden football' without a ball, gracefully performing all the gestures of the game – passing, running, attempting a goal, clapping for the team – until gunfire is heard and they quickly disperse. Forbidden by the Islamic State to watch or play football, these players play in defiance of official rules, performing their gestures and being carried along by them, come what may. One of the most moving films in the series, as Cuauhtémoc Medina has said, *Haram Football* "captures the depth and tenacity of play, but also the importance of a connection with the world for those who live in times of tragedy."[22]

Bruegel and Alÿs provide an inventory of "how the festive impulse arises and persists in conditions inimical to it."[23] Bruegel uses the human figure to suggest these conditions –"material poverty, the body's weight, the self's ingrained aloneness"[24] – and to point to others. Taunting or neglectful figures – the terrifying masked figure in the window at the upper left of the painting, the child in the monk's cowl under the gothic arcade in the middle left, raising a flagellant's whip to a spinning top, and, in the middle right, the woman leaning out to empty a bucket from a ground floor window while a boy with outstretched arms struggles unassisted beside her – ensure the viewer's eye catches the unfriendly darkness amid the exuberance. Alÿs's *Children's Games* is also more than a collection of social repertoires of play. As he has said, each of these games appears "as a means to signify the passing of our own dreams and projects into the future."[25] The inimical conditions surrounding these games can grate against the passing on of dreams, and yet the children play regardless of their circumstances. The feeling for how children play wherever they happen to be, along with their exuberance come what may, is what gives Bruegel's painting and Alÿs's film series such resonance.

Seeing how children play in conflict zones over the years – in Afghanistan, Iraq, and the Democratic Republic of the Congo – Alÿs wonders, "Can a human tragedy be testified to by way of a fictional work?" He warns that terror "fails to be represented."[26] This failure does not spell the end of the art, however, for the children play regardless of terror, sometimes even in the face of it, as we witness poignantly in *Haram Football*. Huizinga quotes from Plato: "What, then, is the right way of living? Life must be lived as play, playing certain games, making sacrifices, singing and dancing, and then a man will be able to propitiate the gods, and defend himself against his enemies, and win in the contest."[27] Whether they are aware of it or not, these children have come to the realization that life, though serious, must be lived as play.

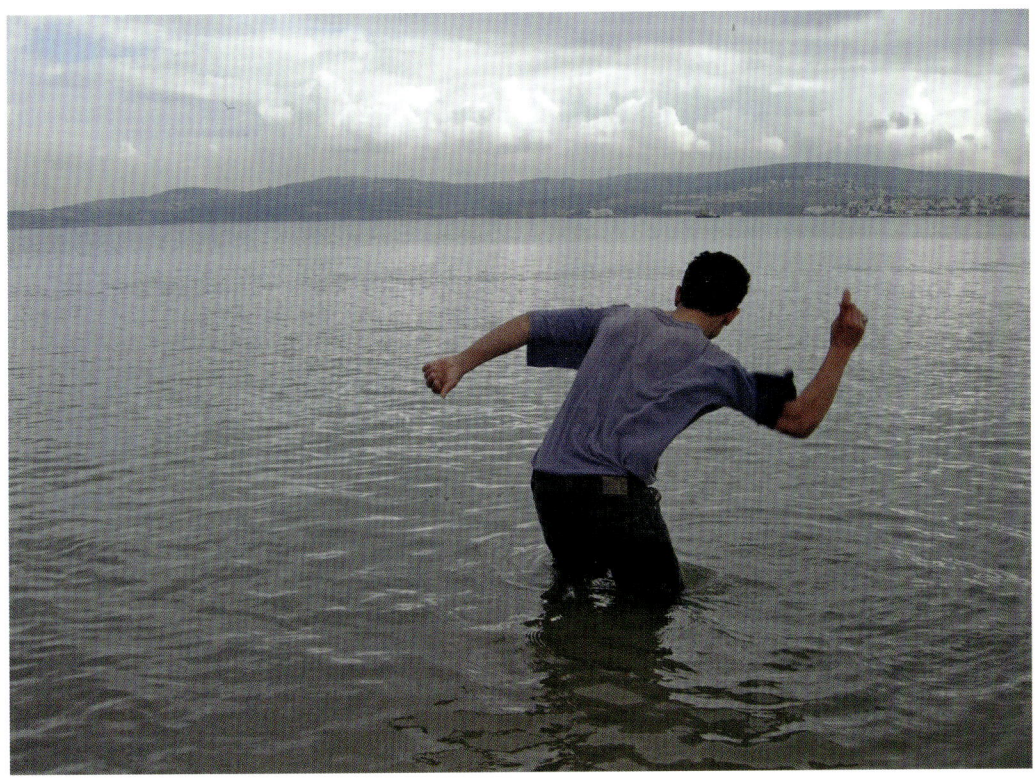

Making of Francis Alÿs, *Children's Game #2: Ricochets*, Tangier, Morocco, 2007 (photo by the artist)

IV

When he was embedded with Kurdish soldiers in Iraq in 2006, at the time he created the film *Sandlines, The Story of History* together with the children from the mountain village near Mosul, Alÿs made a drawing in his notebook of machine guns firing. To the right of the drawing he has written in pencil: "What does it mean to make art while they are destroying Nimrud and Palmyra? If ISIS's logic is 'destroy to exist,' does it mean we ought to create in order to survive?"[28] It would be easy to rush forward in reply, to answer with a resounding yes. Creation emerges between the lines in Alÿs's work, and we see and feel the uplift of creation for human life. Who, though, is the 'we' who is creating? Alÿs ponders what it means to be a creator at a time when to create can literally mean to destroy.

Huizinga anticipated these ruminations. In *Homo Ludens* he observes that as a culture proceeds, "either progressing or regressing, [...] the play-element gradually recedes into the background. [...] But at any moment, even in a highly developed civilization, the play-'instinct' may reassert itself in full force, drowning the individual and the mass in the intoxication of an immense game."[29] The Nazi book burnings and Nuremberg rallies were surely in Huizinga's mind. For today's reader, his lines can bring to mind the forces of ISIS or the destruction of Nimrud and Palmyra. Whatever the case, when creation literally means to destroy, the freedom of the play-'instinct' is wholly perverted, pressed into service by a force which drowns "the individual and the mass in the intoxication of an immense game."[30]

The freedom of art to emerge between the lines and to change is necessary for the existence of art, as well as the existence of ourselves. By working collaboratively, by relying on the viewer to constitute the work of art, Alÿs opens creation beyond himself to take in whenever we happen to be, come what may. This body of work is a lesson in not seeing once and for all. Alÿs answers back to ISIS's logic of 'destroy to exist' with a resounding 'create to exist' that includes every collaborator in his work and every viewer of it.

The grace of Alÿs's creations extends to their political import. He has asked, "how can art remain politically significant without assuming a doctrinal standpoint or aspiring to become social activism?"[31] These works invite our participation but also undermine the power of the gaze by an instability that keeps the viewer from settling into fixed positions of seeing or meaning. As Alÿs has said, he wants creations that "can shake up [our] assumptions about the way things are, that can destabilize and open up, for just an instant – in a flash – a different vision of the situation, as if from the inside."[32] This is how creation can be political: it can "travel as an anecdote or fable"; it can spread like stories; it can disclose visions of the world which the world as we know it has prevented us from seeing until now.

Through the act of constituting these creations and passing them on we transmit their qualities forward in time. Thus we vouchsafe art and storytelling, poetics and politics, hope and freedom. Thus we continue the invention and re-invention of these essential qualities every day. Perhaps we are now ready to affirm that these projects form a single narrative, which is: human life exists between the lines of societal structures and strictures, and where there is human life, there is hope. In his essay "The Play of Art," Gadamer asks: "What can the picture tell us of the context of our lives?"[33] These pictures by Alÿs and his collaborators tell us there is hope for us, too, if we invent hope every day.

Notes

1. "Russell Ferguson in Conversation with Francis Alÿs" (2007). In: Russell Ferguson, Cuauhtémoc Medina & Jean Fisher (eds.), *Francis Alÿs*. London: Phaidon. 42.

2. Johan Huizinga (1949). *Homo Ludens: A Study of the Play-Element in Culture*. Trans. Richard Francis Carrington Hull. London: Routledge & Kegan Paul. 13. Huizinga fought for the subtitle 'A Study of the Play-Element of Culture' over the given 'in Culture,' since it was not his objective "to define the place of play among all the other manifestations of culture, but rather to ascertain how far culture itself bears the characteristics of play." Johan Huizinga (1949). Op. cit., 2. An historian writing in the mid-1930s, Huizinga would have been keenly aware of what befalls when culture loses the character of free and voluntary play.

3. Roger Caillois (2001). *Man, Play and Games*. Trans. Meyer Barash. Urbana, IL: University of Illinois Press.

4. "Russell Ferguson in Conversation with Francis Alÿs." Op. cit., 55.

5. Email from Francis Alÿs to Saul Anton, October 6, 2003. Quoted in Saul Anton (2003). "One More Step." *Parkett* 69, 36.

6. "Russell Ferguson in Conversation with Francis Alÿs." Op. cit., 18.

7. Ibid., 18.

8. Eyal Weizman (2010). "The 1:1 Map." In: Mark Godfrey, Klaus Biesenbach and Kerryn Greenberg (eds.), *Francis Alÿs: A Story of Deception*. London: Tate Publishing. 175.

9. Ibid, 176.

10. Francis Alÿs and Cuauhtéhmoc Medina in *Francis Alÿs: A Story of Deception*. Op. cit., 143.

11. Hans-Georg Gadamer (1986). "The Play of Art." In: Robert Bernasconi (ed.), *The Relevance of the Beautiful and Other Essays*. Cambridge: Cambridge University Press. 126.

12. "Russell Ferguson in Conversation with Francis Alÿs." Op. cit., 26.

13. Hans-Georg Gadamer (1986). Op. cit., 126.

14. Maco Magazine Corp. (1955). *The Family of Man: The Greatest Photographic Exhibition of All Time – 503 Pictures from 68 Countries*. New York: published for MoMA.

15. "Play generates novel ways of dealing with the environment, most of which lead nowhere but some of which turn out to be useful." Patrick Bateson and Paul Martin (2013). *Play, Playfulness, Creativity and Innovation* Cambridge: Cambridge University Press. 4.

16. *Francis Alÿs: spel zonder grenzen* (2022), dir. Pieter Verbiest and Bertrand Lafontaine.

17. Johan Huizinga (1949). Op. cit., 7–8.

18. Hans-Georg Gadamer (1994). *Truth and Method*. Trans. Joel Weinsheimer and Donald G. Marshall. New York: Continuum. 102.

19. Wendy Russell, Malcolm MacLean and Emily Ryall (eds.) (2018). *The Philosophy of Play as Life*. London: Taylor and Francis. 2.

20. Ibid.

21. Hans-Georg Gadamer (1986), "Image and Gesture." In: *The Relevance of the Beautiful*. Op. cit., 79.

22. Cuauhtémoc Medina (2020). "Un juego entre ruinas/Playing Among the Ruins." In: *Francis Alÿs: Salam Tristesse, Irak, 2016–2020*. Bogotá: Museo Nacional de Colombia. 19. This catalogue is dedicated by Alÿs to the children of Iraq.

23. Edward Snow (1997). *Inside Bruegel: The Play of Images in Children's Games*. New York: North Point Press, Farrar, Straus and Giroux. 57.

24. Ibid.

25. Francis Alÿs in *Francis Alÿs: A Story of Deception*. Op. cit., 164.

26. Francis Alÿs's embed diary. Tuesday, November 1, 2016. In *Francis Alÿs: Salam Tristesse*. Op. cit., 7.

27. Plato, *Laws*, 803–4, quoted in Johan Huizinga (1949). Op. cit., 212. See also Gavin Ardley (July 1967). *The Role of Play in the Philosophy of Plato*. Philosophy 42 (161), 226–44.

28. The reader will see that the second sentence is abbreviated in the drawing. The entire sentence, which is included here, appears in Alÿs's embed diary, Friday, November 4, 2016. In: *Francis Alÿs: Salam Tristesse*. Op. cit., 8.

29. Johan Huizinga (1949). Op. cit., 47.

30. Some five years later, in Johan Huizinga (April 1943). "History Changing Form". *Journal of the History of Ideas* 4 (2), 217–223, Huizinga witnesses with foreboding the mechanization of all social life. "Once *numbers* reign supreme in our society," he warned, "there will be no story left to tell, no images for history to evoke" (223).

31. Francis Alÿs in "Russell Ferguson in Conversation with Francis Alÿs," Op. cit., 40. See also Francis Alÿs (2006). "Fragments of a Conversation in Buenos Aires." In: *A Story of Deception: Patagonia 2003–2006*. Buenos Aires: Fundación Eduardo F. Constantini. 82.

32. Francis Alÿs in "Russell Ferguson in Conversation with Francis Alÿs." Op. cit., 40.

33. Hans-Georg Gadamer (1986). "The Play of Art". Op. cit., 89.

Not a Playground

Rodrigo Pérez de Arce Antoncic*

I

Play, observed Roger Caillois, is essentially an unproductive endeavor. Because it is not geared towards the construction, or, more broadly, change of the world, when play ceases, everything falls back into place. It jolts the rhythms of ordinary life through a miraculous parenthesis and then vanishes from the scene.

Spanning continents and cultures, Francis Alÿs has so far portrayed more than thirty children's games. Remarkably, none of them unfolds within the bounds of what we would consider a proper 'playground.' In his narrative, a bunch of joyful children of all continents turned whatever places they seized into lively playgrounds, probably shunning the established ones. Or perhaps they had none at hand. Their exploits left no significant material tokens, only endearing personal and collective memories.

Such a *détournement* (to borrow from the Situationists) – a willful turning-around of reality for the purpose of sheer recreation – was the common practice of childhood until the advent of the modern playground, when this subversion of ordinary experience became somewhat previsualized by professionals and experts.

* Rodrigo Pérez de Arce Antoncic is an architect and Professor at the Pontificia Universidad Católica de Chile.

I will outline how the purpose-made playground, an urban artefact designed and equipped for the ludic practices of children, came to be conceived as the rightful setting for such experiences. Its assertive configurations wrested childhood play away from invisibility, making its presence felt – even vicariously – in a tangible way as urban artefacts do, both during playtime and after. This account will therefore suggest a counterpoint between the universe of the formal playground and the fields of spontaneous play such as displayed in Alÿs's narrative.

There was a time – which gained momentum in the first half of the last century – when childhood play decisively entered the professional arena, adding another vital design task to be mastered in the fostering of the modern habitat. Henceforth, ad hoc, sometimes bizarre purpose-made ensembles, mainly conceived by architects, sometimes by artists or landscape professionals, aimed to host those multifarious and essentially unpredictable ludic impulses. By then, the doctrine of spatial zoning – that is, the slotting of activities in discrete places according to rational criteria – was well entrenched, with its sponsorship of functional enclaves, so that the practices of play were accordingly assigned specific – often exclusive – locations.

The official reckoning with children's play gained an interesting and somewhat enhanced priority in Western countries in the wake of the Second World War. It was motivated by varied and sometimes contrasting aims, mostly concordant with the social agendas endorsed by the welfare state. However, the playground agenda was also compelled, above all – and consistently so – by the imperative of taking children away from the street.[1] When probing into the formal playground, our focus must shift somewhat away from the players and instead toward the design professionals to whom society entrusted the ideation and design of those specialized enclaves.

II

Apart from some minor details, Alÿs's miscellaneous games have a certain atemporal status, universal dimensions, and a surprising spatial ubiquity. Most of them feel familiar, as if childhood shares so many – almost identical – impulses worldwide.

We can safely add that they elude any form of spatial planning other than the impromptu vectors shared by the players, when fully immersed in play. Such fleeting constellations may bring out preferences for specific physical settings, perhaps even reiterate their ludic use, but even then, the light touch involved in children's games would conspire against leaving behind any enduring traces.

What about these settings? Most of them seem to fit that broad and diffuse domain of the 'informal,' places bereft of firm outlines, dusty, irregular, somewhat rough or unfinished, certainly removed from expected standards of 'urbanization.'

However, sometimes official sanctions are bestowed upon impromptu playgrounds: thus Steen Eiler Rasmussen describes how the London Moorfields – a de facto urban commons – evolved through custom and stubborn reiteration into an embryonic people's park by the early seventeenth century.[2] Other cities and other times witnessed similar transferences, from the loosely defined to the officially sanctioned, with both approaches achieved through spatial designation, the establishment of formal patterns, and administrative enforcement.

The light material touch involved in children's games makes such consolidation unlikely, but the world of play is both immensely rich and nuanced. Caillois's conceptual distinction of ludic genres, which he designates *paideia* and *ludus* (otherwise loosely described as 'play' and 'game'), comes in handy in clarifying the transactions made between the ad hoc and the designed playground.[3]

Paideia is spontaneous. Bereft of established rules, it rests upon the illusory 'as if,' hence upon provisional constellations. 'Illusion' – Huizinga reminds us – derives from 'in ludere,' 'being in the game.' *Ludus* spells out its rules, appeals to specified and agreed-upon relations, therefore furnishing legal and explicit frameworks. Both emerge from equally arbitrary assumptions, but only *ludus* makes history. It perpetuates itself through reiteration. One example is how modern sport consolidated its neat and very specific ludic grounds, also construing its chronologies, records, and lasting myths. *Paideia* just reinvents itself relentlessly, even if through subtle variations.[4]

Paideia, however, is in Caillois's conception the cradle of play, a true laboratory. Its embryonic practices may even consolidate through the acquisition of a formal set of rules. It then enters the ranks of *ludus* in a transformation which often involves the formalization of the grounds.

This transformation has been described by Norbert Elias, who arrived at the issue of play when inquiring into how societies forge social conventions. Elias observed how certain English ballgames that were originally performed upon loosely defined fields developed into formal sports, through shared agreements that led their transition from "pastimes" into "sports."[5] These conventions, which he conceived in line with the "civilizing process," embraced the notion of the team, the numbers and roles of players, the rules of the game, the enforcement of a playing time, issues of attire, and the technical definition of the equipment, in addition to – and significantly so – the formal and material definition of the playing field in its geometry, topography, scale, size, and orientation.

The establishment of formal sports intensified enormously in England mainly because, he thought, English society was introducing certain rules of behavior to help resolve its internal conflicts and violence. In addition to this, it was strengthening the democratic rules of engagement in Parliament. In fact, the House of Commons itself embodied the agonistic/ludic confrontation of government and opposition, since seats were positioned face-to-face and members only played by the rules.

III

The exploits captured by Alÿs's lens represent a more recurrent picture of how and where play is performed in modern societies than the sum of ludic activities funneled into formal playgrounds, architectural schemes and carefully scripted situations. Children never regard a place as a tabula rasa, one devoid of qualities, however precarious these qualities may be. In their minds, places are as bountiful and subtle as the fissures in the pavements, turned into a motif for a rhythmic and evanescent urban dance in *Children's Game #23: Step on a Crack* (2020). A girl from Hong Kong makes a world of her own, seemingly aloof with regard to daily routines, but she nevertheless thrives in being so immersed for she realizes that she is present in a shared, physical space. Maneuvering within the crowd, she negotiates her movements without clashing with other people's bodies while she at the same time turns incidents along her route into obstacles to be sorted out rhythmically. She is not concerned with arriving sooner at her destination, but with turning the mundane itinerary into a pleasurable event. In doing so, she probes the city's resilient surface and reveals its many imperfections. Hers is not an intellectual assessment of things made, even less an aesthetic appreciation of the architectonic fabric of the city, but a sort of celebration through an intense and very physical entanglement with the urban place and its anonymous inhabitants.

Similar attitudes may drive children to snatch the latent opportunities offered by a given scenario, even if a daunting one, as is the case with Lubumbashi's colossal slag heap when it is taken over by a group of boys determined to test its slopes through a high-speed and hazardous experiment, in *Children's Game #29: La roue* (2021). The mound's stark bareness does not attenuate their interest. On the contrary, they reckon that in presenting the experiment so effectively, the roughness of the environment highlights its epic overtones.

Clearly, their action is entirely futile: it changes nothing. It improves nothing, except that henceforth they will most probably perceive the massive slag heap differently, perhaps affectionately, the way a mountaineer appreciates the conquered summit from afar, not as a mere 'accident' but as a singularly charged place.

Neither are children indifferent to the urban labyrinth made of the shells of an abandoned housing project. Once taken over by Mexican boys and girls, the somewhat forbidding site is reawakened through a hide-and-seek game of mirrors in *Children's Game #15: Espejos* (2013). Vaguely recalling home – either as promise (as unfinished dwellings can do) or as a doomed expectation – this expansive setting offers nonetheless enough scope for their protracted experiments. Children turn the empty cluster into a field of chance where each wall counts as a potential refuge. Light and shade interact, above all through the 'lethal' reflections cast by each mirror. Alertness is called for throughout their play, for this is meant to be a life-or-death confrontation.

As if wresting the secrets of the *genius loci*, players bring to the fore some of the site's innate qualities such as sonority, scale, texture, topography, visual range, materiality, and so on. They perform selected traits in their ludic experiments, it would seem, much like instruments would do in a symphony. Theirs is definitely a high-intensity interaction with architecture, and one that had not even been anticipated within the imaginary scripts of the architectural project.

These impromptu choices contradict common assumptions. Neither the street, nor the slag heap or the concrete shells of the abandoned houses conform to the expectations of softness, friendliness, colorfulness,

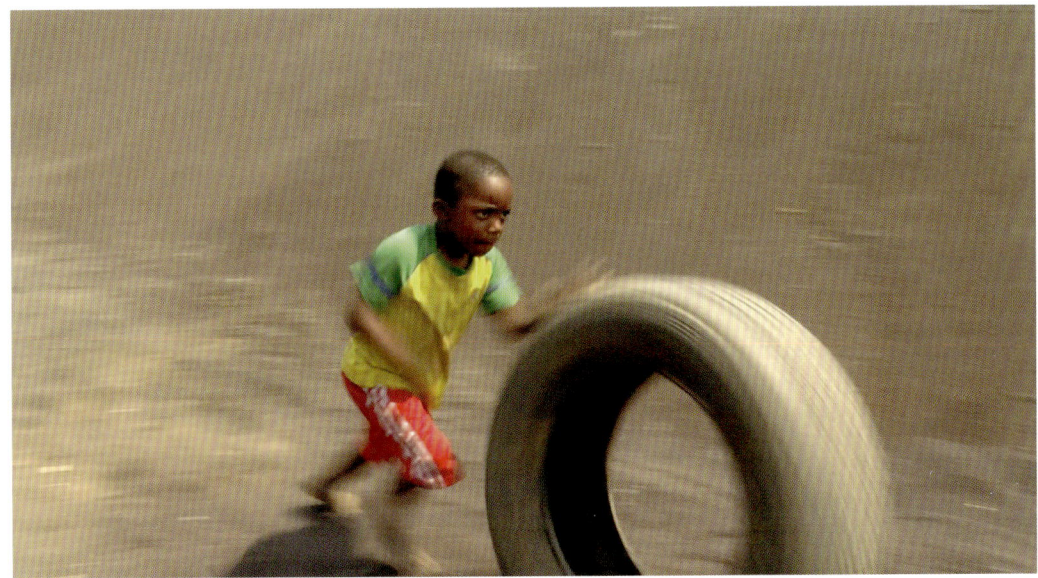

Francis Alÿs, *Children's Game #29: La roue*, Lubumbashi, Democratic Republic of the Congo, 2021 (still)

cuteness, or smallness so often associated with childhood. Unlike the offerings of Disney World and its derivations, these scenarios, which were obviously never tailored to the needs of children, invite their face-to-face interplay with the rough facts of life. Here the alchemists' *genii* – barely hidden in each child – reciprocate, turning reality over.

Added to the enhancement that play brings into the appreciation of reality and the somewhat mischievous element in *paideia*, there is an overwhelming sense of urgency. The pressures of the here and now – so common to these experiments – suggest paradoxical affinities with the experiences of warfare, where the most subtle element on the ground counts as a matter of serious concern. In play and warfare alike, subtle attentiveness brings out tactical priorities. This makes commanding the site of action a matter of sheer survival.

IV

How can anyone design a children's playground? Given children's prodigious inventiveness, is there any need to do so? And if so, what are its formal, material, spatial, or topological premises?

The conception of formal playgrounds for unstructured or spontaneous play is not at all straightforward: while *ludus* calls for a faithful reproduction of its templates such as reflected, for example, in the sport field's neat outlines, no such path is supplied by *paideia*, which is bereft of prescriptions. Paradoxically, *ludus* often obliterates the scope for invention, for it commands a precise reproduction of its grounds. Contrariwise, despite the inherent and almost ontological contradiction about shaping the grounds for random and unpredictable events, *paideia* offers an unbounded range for creativity. This proclivity must account for the keen interest that has been awakened in design professionals within this field.

It is not surprising, then, that much like laboratories, playgrounds briefly sponsored a wide range of formal and behavioral experiments. Thus, for example, their plastic and compositional formations were sometimes assumed to recast certain compact urban formats long abandoned by the functionalist doctrine. Because playgrounds were accepted as heterotopias or places of exception, they could invoke alternative spatial arrays, re-edit 'primitive' formats, configure landscapes of memory, or perhaps cast powerful spatial archetypes. Indeed, play forms indistinctly convene past or future scenarios, as observed by Caillois, who highlighted how play could either anticipate events in "serious life," as if rehearsing them, or else recast past events through the reactivation of long forgotten practices. Unsurprisingly, the playground was often perceived as a sort of incubator.

With the advent of the 1950s, an outpouring of fascinating proposals arose around the idea of shaping the grounds for the illusory 'as if' embedded in the very notion of *paideia*. Unfortunately, this was to be just a fleeting moment of opportunity, for serious considerations about safety reduced the scope of playground design just a few decades later.

Against such a manifest range of options, how could choices be made? Should the designer go for flat or complex surfaces? Mono-material or materially and texturally composite components? Fuzzy or simple structures? Single foci, or multifocal organizations? "[W]e cannot conceive of civilization today if we withdraw the child—ourselves—from its built counter form: the city," claimed architect Aldo Van Eyck in 1962. He continued, in his very personal style, "Nor can we come to terms with cities if we cut ourselves from the force—that alone—can humanize them: imagination. Nor for that matter, can we open the doors of imagination without shaking hands with the artist."[6]

Imagination was the binding force that kept Van Eyck's triad of *the child, the city, and the artist* in a state of perpetual interplay. One should stress the priority that this noted architect assigns to the ludic subject.

Because playgrounds ought to forge settings where imagination reigns supreme, it was not surprising that many artists were attracted to the topic.

Sculptor Isamu Noguchi's *Play Mountain* was to be his first pronouncement on the topic. It was to be a massive mound inscribed within Manhattan's super-urban grid, "an enhanced area for children's play," as he said,[7] a monumental piece ready to embrace the most direct interface an artist can imagine between their work and the public. Although stylized and emphatically geometric, in its invitation to frolic with the force of gravity, the monumental fabrication somewhat recalls Lubumbashi's slag heap. Noguchi's would have been a more benign colossus, to be sure, but in fostering a world apart through its emphasis on otherness, it equally induced children to fly in wonderment. Highlighting the rhythms of nature, the bulky playground also celebrated the seasons, offering water games in summer and sledding and snow games in winter.

It is evident that formality is a critical element in *Play Mountain*, unlike Lubumbashi's heap, whose form simply betrays a pragmatic logic about how to accumulate waste material. Yet more fundamentally, its importance as a project – a projectile, a shot into the future that anticipated certain actions and orchestrated possible choreographies which only reality can sanction – confirms the ontological gulf that distinguishes the 'as found' from the 'custom-made.'

Playing with gravity is surely a recondite choice: the screaming children, romping in snowy landscapes in *Children's Game #33: Schneespiele* (2022), make its excitement abundantly clear. Topography is also present – albeit in a more subdued and intimate register – in *Children's Game #8: Marbles* (2010), in which children pay close attention to minute ground inflections. Marbles probe these ground inflections the same way children do with their own bodies when sliding or rolling down. The point is precisely that topography can call out for play, unleashing its immanent and irresistible potentials, as proven by a whole range of playgrounds which are fashioned upon this simple premise.

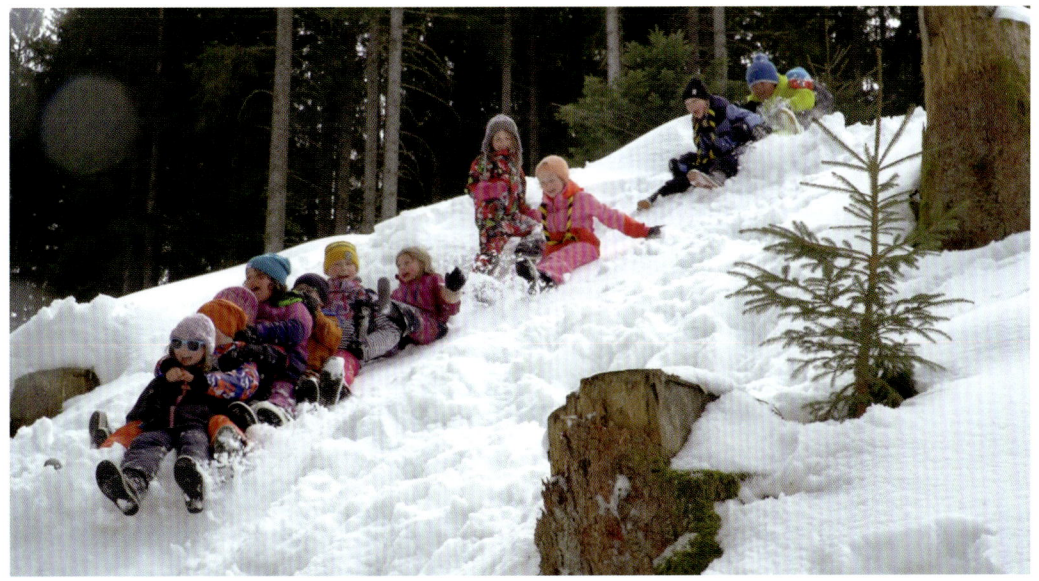

Francis Alÿs, *Children's Game #33: Schneespiele*, Engelberg, Switzerland, 2022 (still)

Playground designers often appealed to abstraction to achieve their aims. Moreover, in the so-called play sculptures, artists found an intensity of interaction between the work of art and the public which exceeded the merely visual engagement; something direct and unprejudiced, yet subtle, and, in a way, quite judicious.

V

Artificial mounds, gravitational fields, or topographic folds may sometimes echo impromptu play spaces. Yet other, somewhat bizarre and unexpected reverberations between these domains were embedded in what was originally christened the 'junk playground.'

Children's Game #19: Haram Football (2017) brings into the scene the sad squalor caused by warfare in what seems to be a well-to-do district of Mosul, Iraq. A devastated urban landscape sets the scene for this surreal street contest. Engrossed in play, children seem oblivious to the depressing background: such is play's enchanting ability to configure a world apart.

Decades earlier, while visiting the Ruhr region in Germany, the architect Alfred Traschel recalled how, against all expectations, those he called "children of the debris, barefooted and in rags" played with fragments of wreckage upon the mountains of rubble amassed in the aftermath of the war. Wrenching joyfulness from dereliction while claiming their space in such unlikely scenarios, they inadvertently offered a glimmer of hope.

The element of chance and inventiveness forged the idea of the 'adventure playground.' It was often a site of randomness, indeterminacy, disorder, also precariousness, as if mimicking shanties from underdeveloped settings. Its original invention in the hands of Danish landscape architect Theodor Sörensen contemplated a bare site, only supplied with building materials and a storeroom, the whole ensemble somewhat replicating a building site, which was his original source of inspiration. Earth banks and lines of trees kept its perpetual disorder out of sight. In their relentless and open-ended action, children construed and deconstructed scenarios upon the bare field, assuming more risks than would be nowadays acceptable, while following no scripts. In embracing indeterminacy, the adventure playground was moving farther away from the conundrum involved in prefiguring play modes through fixed built forms.

The formula spread to London and other destinations, often finding its way on to bombed or derelict sites. The tenuous shacks built on the adventure playground formed a curious counterpoint to the recently built massive housing blocks. The resonance was unintended, for the latter were not aiming at quoting the fragile landscapes of 'underdevelopment.' Still, the assemblages betrayed certain levels of spontaneity and vitality that were far removed from the tightly controlled planned developments common to the 'advanced' societies that often hosted these initiatives: small heterotopias embedded in rational and well-ordered urban districts.

VI

In 1960, Alfred Traschel and Alfred Ledermann published the seminal "Playground and Recreation Centres", a fully illustrated compendium which reviewed the state of the art in the provision of playground facilities, in an era which many consider its heyday. Such provision was then mainly entrusted to the state or to local authorities. Planning ludic spaces for the various ages of childhood was examined with the aim of assigning the right spaces to each age group. Its emphasis upon discrete special enclaves, optimized through specialized settings, affirmed the practice of zoning. Having reached consensus upon the ills of the 'roadway,' street planners relentlessly attempted to recast the social areas in these grounds. Principal aims were to segregate pedestrians from vehicular traffic, thus averting danger and avoiding noxious pollution. Children were often recalled as the ones most vulnerable and affected worst. Street play was invoked as an almost emblematic issue that had to be resolved and set apart from such congested and unhealthy environments. Their removal into softer and safe environments was a shared assumption.

Similar exploits to the above-mentioned street games were prominently displayed by architects Alison and Peter Smithson with the aid of Nigel Henderson's memorable photographs of street play in London's East End. Here there was a vivid portrayal of the street as arena. Why should architects resort to such vignettes in their inquiries about urban design? One reason was their keen interest in the ordinary and the everyday: play was a beautiful expression of the 'as found.' Another one was the element of interplay they detected between those children and the fabric of the average London street where they performed, which revealed a chance element and a loose-fit relation between site and action. These could supply interesting keys in the formulation of congenial urban patterns, and so was the need for a communal arena as symbolic fulcrum. "In the uninhibited organization of the children's games we are seeing a valid pattern," the Smithsons stated in 1967, "and this is an indication of a freer form of organization."[8] Highlighting their interest in the subject of play, their street diagrams attempted to capture evanescent ludic choreographies, with the aim of reinforcing their urban contexts. Somewhat contradictorily, however, in devising new urban patterns in their Golden Lane Scheme, they removed the ludic arena entirely from the street and relegated it to a rather conventional playground that was embedded in the grounds and cushioned in greenery. Their design option in fact recalled a generalized expectation. "*Creating playgrounds and community centres and green areas for recreation with quiet places and footpaths away from the roar of traffic is a task with which the urban planner is confronted*," Ledermann and Traschel stated in 1960.[9] 'Greenery' was a more suitable ambiance for kids than hard-edged environments.

Such enforced removal from the street did not go unchallenged. Jane Jacobs notoriously decried the havoc caused by the heavy top-down re-ordering of life in cities as was practiced by the New York local authorities in their massive redevelopments. The street was for her the place that brought the greatest range of human activities and actors into a shared scene. Bernard Rudofsky, for whom the modern playground was a repressive tool of "metal cages and concrete bunkers," was also a stern supporter of the street as the one environment where children could gain insights into life. Many others like John Brinckerhoff Jackson, Herman Hertzberger, Jean Duvignaud and Henri Lefebvre reclaimed the child's ludic rights to ordinary urban spaces, common rights that were so menaced by the institution of the playground and its own agendas, albeit well-meaning, of social exclusion. It is to this group of thinkers and writers that Alÿs most firmly belongs, since he makes visible what resists the forces of sanitation and social isolation: *Children's Game #23: Step on a Crack*, *Children's Game #19: Haram Football*, and *Children's Game #1: Caracoles* (1999) unfold upon hard, unyielding road surfaces but they fully contradict the universal precept that children should be kept away from the street altogether.

Players always construe a *temenos*, a sacred ground within which certain types of rules abide. Such construction may be elastic, even loosely defined, as frequently happens in *paideia*, but it is nevertheless indispensable in fostering the world apart that the act of play requires. This *temenos* sometimes crystalizes in neat geometric configurations, which trace parallels with ritual spaces. These may be evanescent, as when children draw with chalk upon a pavement but whether recurring to visible markings or not, children can turn just about any space into a playground. They leave behind happy memories like smiles in the city's face. This is what comes about with Alÿs's films.

How far removed all this is from certain designers' visions that gained much currency in the past century, such as the one embedded in Le Corbusier's 1938 vignette *Jeu, Ville Radieuse*. There, a green landscape traversed by Cartesian arabesques is permeated by citizens at leisure: their bodies resting by water pools on the rooftops, engrossed in frantic play on the various sport fields in the park, swimming, frolicking on sand banks either upon the ground or on roof terraces ... In this luminous setting, conflicts were simply eradicated, for while play reigned supreme, it was all preordained. Geometry and precision ruled over spontaneity and disorder. In mastering leisure time, the *Ville Radieuse* set a significant precedent for disciplining the rebellious play instinct. Never had architects been so keen to control that sphere of life. Since then, the playground and the impromptu playing field have been competing as rightful ludic arenas.

Notes

1. I have argued this issue more extensively in Rodrigo Pérez de Arce (2018). *City of Play: An Architectural and Urban History of Recreation and Leisure*. London: Bloomsbury Visual Arts; also in Manuel Borja Villel & Teresa Velasquez (eds.) (2014). *Playgrounds. Reinventing the Square*. Madrid: Reina Sofia Museum, Siruela.

2. Steen Eiler Rasmussen (1983). *London: The Unique City*. Cambridge, MA: MIT Press.

3. Roger Caillois (2001). *Man, Play and Games*. Trans. Meyer Barash. Urbana, IL: University of Illinois Press.

4. Johan Huizinga (1949). *Homo Ludens: A Study of the Play-Element in Culture*. Trans. Richard Francis Carrington Hull. London: Routledge & Kegan Paul.

5. Norbert Elias & Eric Dunning (1986). *Quest for Excitement: Sport and Leisure in the Civilizing Process*. Oxford: Basil Blackwell.

6. Aldo Van Eyck, Francis Strauven (ed.) (2008). *The Child, the City and the Artist: An Essay on Architecture. The In-between Realm*. Amsterdam: SUN Publishers. 18–20.

7. Isamu Noguchi (1987). *The Isamu Noguchi Garden Museum Catalogue*. New York: Harry N. Abrams. 144.

8. Peter Smithson (1967). *Urban Structuring Studies of Alison and Peter Smithson*. London: Studio Vista. 10.

9. Alfred Ledermann & Alfred Traschel (1960). *Creative playgrounds and recreational centres*. New York: Frederick A. Praeger. 26.

A Space to Play

Zeynep Kubat*

I

Francis Alÿs is a world traveller, a flaneur, a nomad.[1] Or, at least, that is the standard interpretation for his work.[2] This more homogeneous discourse around the artist's practice is sometimes quite restrictive or even problematic, because it implies a blindness to borders. Ignoring borders and border experiences is a symptom of global capitalist politics, whereas Alÿs is critically responding to such politics throughout his oeuvre. The artist shows us how to recognize and cross borders with the hope of creating encounters. In doing so, Alÿs explores the political potential of play, a quest that culminates in his long-term project *Children's Games* (1999-ongoing). Play becomes the space where humor, wonder, and freedom can emerge, despite social rules or societal straitjackets. Our drive to play generates social connection and can shape a community, outside the lines of any type of frontier.

II

Francis Alÿs's works are well known for their poetical politics. One of the most recognized features of his work is the use of lines as a metaphor to explore issues around national identity, migration, and globalization.

* Zeynep Kubat is a curator and art writer based in Brussels, Belgium.

They highlight how people's movements are restricted and controlled by governments and other institutions. For *The Loop* (1997), for instance, he travelled to the InSite Biennial that takes place between Tijuana and San Diego. Invited art professionals, collectors, and artists comfortably tread this border zone. Outside the art event exists a dark reality, in which people face death or abuse while crossing the border to the U.S. To address the bias of the biennial and the racism of U.S. policies, he avoided the easy route and took a 35-day voyage through nineteen cities in different countries to reach the event. In *The Green Line* (2004), a similar interrogation of border politics, the artist walked over the Green Line that divides Jerusalem in two parts. After the 1948 Arab-Israeli War, this demarcation line divided the city into a Palestinian zone and an Israeli zone. Even though it's not a legal frontier, the Israeli government has been using it as their de facto national border ever since. This occupation has turned into decades of structural violence against Palestinians up until today. Alluding to its name and the green pencil with which it was supposedly drawn during the Armistice Agreements of 1949, Alÿs walked with a leaky can of green paint over the part that runs through Jerusalem. 58 liters of green paint were used to trace 24 kilometers. The action was based on a previous performance in São Paolo in 1995, where he walked with a leaky can of blue paint through the city. This work became exemplary for his poetic approach in political issues, as the artist expressed it himself: "Sometimes doing something poetic can become political and sometimes doing something political can become poetic."[3]

Nevertheless, many writers, such as curator Mark Godfrey, describe the practice of Alÿs as the attempt to create a "vision of a world without borders," which is exactly the false promise of globalized capitalism.[4] Such common interpretations of Alÿs's work engender readings of borders as things that can be abolished by their transformation into an artwork. The dream of globalization is proposed as a harmonious connection between different nations on socio-economic and cultural levels through neoliberal market practices but proved to be, in reality, a gateway for extractivist capitalism. In his writings, anthropologist Arjun Appadurai explains how globalization consists of multiple "things" that move in "global flows." These things in motion are currencies and commodified goods, as well as objects, persons, discourses, images, cultural phenomena, and ideas. They do not "flow" together simultaneously in one connected network, but in lagged relationships of *disjuncture*, as each thing is differently valued everywhere. Women or queer persons do not receive the same rights in all countries. Visual culture circulates in a way incongruous with consumable goods. Discourses and ideas are accepted or refused depending on local cultures and values. Appadurai explains how "these disjunctures themselves precipitate various kinds of problems and frictions in different local situations. Indeed, it is the various vectors characterizing this world-in-motion that produce fundamental problems of livelihood, equity, suffering, justice, and governance."[5] In other words, the movement of every human product or form of expression is directed by limitations, rules, authorities, lines, and borders.

If we understand how these disjunctures in global flows help create the problematic policies around borders, as part of a world that self-perpetuates deep inequality, such utopian visions become the opposite of being socially critical or political. Attempting to picture this impossible world without borders through art may sound hopeful, but it is in Appadurai's view an imaginary fugue for the fundamental problems. Border-blindness numbs a proper understanding of the realities around borderlands[6] and ignores the political, socio-economic, and cultural differences that exist between people from privileged identities and those who live in areas of conflict, colonization, and/or poverty. The approach of Alÿs is centered around an *awareness* of borders, rather than a utopian world *without* them, though this element is overlooked in many interpretations. His work creates an imagination that creates bridges and crosses borders as a reaction to capitalist fabulations.

The film *Don't Cross the Bridge Before You Get to the River* (2008), for instance, aptly illustrates his position. Alÿs wanted to create a symbolical bridge between Morocco and Spain by crossing a strongly contested geographical border, the Strait of Gibraltar, with a line of boats. He invited a group of Moroccan children and a group of Spanish children to form a line in the sea, each departing from the coast of their own country, holding small boats made from shoes. The hypothetical experiment revolved around an attempt to see if they could meet in the middle and create a crossing for a place where many migrants' and refugees' paths end. For Alÿs, "the Strait of Gibraltar seemed like the obvious place to illustrate this contradiction of our times: how can one promote global economy and at the same time limit the global flow of people across continents?"[7]

III

Ever since Alÿs came across a Mexican boy kicking a bottle up a steep street in Mexico City and saw two kids in Tangier skipping stones by the sea, his fascination for children playing became an important drive for what would galvanize into the project *Children's Games* as we know it today. These two chance encounters were *Children's Game #1* and *#2*, respectively, *Caracoles* (1999) and *Ricochets* (2007). In the years that followed, Alÿs researched which 'analog' games were played by children in public spaces, away from the influence of the digital realm, and came across a variety of playful encounters between children all over the world. Even if this growing collection of children's games is presented as a search for something that is universal in a fragmented and divided world, or something that connects many different cultures despite the disturbances in global flows, the project is not an illustration of a world without borders. Quite the contrary: it's a confrontation with them, a search for ways to perpetually cross them, with poetry and politics.

Even the children's games have their own demarcation lines, symbolic borders, and rules in their own universe. The socio-political demarcations of exclusion that Alÿs detects so well throughout his oeuvre are represented within the confined 'space' of the game, too. Firstly, the explicit politics of most *Games* are intrinsic to the situation in which the children play. Many videos were filmed in regions marked by political or religious conflict, poverty, and forms of colonization or occupation. One cannot film apolitically in such contexts, which made the choice of the artist for these spaces carefully considered. A clear example of this is *Children's Game #10: Papalote* (2011). Children play with kites in war-torn Afghanistan, a country that was at the time occupied during years on end by Taliban, Daesh, and the U.S. Army. In *Children's Game #29: La roue* (2021), the wry fact that children in Lubumbashi are playing on the same hills of cobalt that they must extract creates a bitter connection between child's play and child labor. Despite their daily lives being restricted by social, economic, political, and religious borderlines, the children are still driven to play, together.

The political issues at stake are not just the contexts in which the children play, but also intrinsic to the social rules of the games. In some parts of the world, not only the children but also the games themselves are limited by poverty, violence, war, or other social factors. For instance, in *Children's Game #19: Haram Football* (2017), we see how playing football became an act of resistance for children in Mosul. A group of boys are playing the game without a ball, only two years after thirteen children were executed for watching football on television by the then ruling Daesh forces. Another important aspect here is that the game was only played by boys. As Alÿs observed in his notebook, many children's games are early practices of gender segregation.[8] Another example of this is *Children's Game #28: Nzango* (2021), a game that can only be played by girls and women, and which has even grown into a national sport in the Democratic Republic of the Congo.

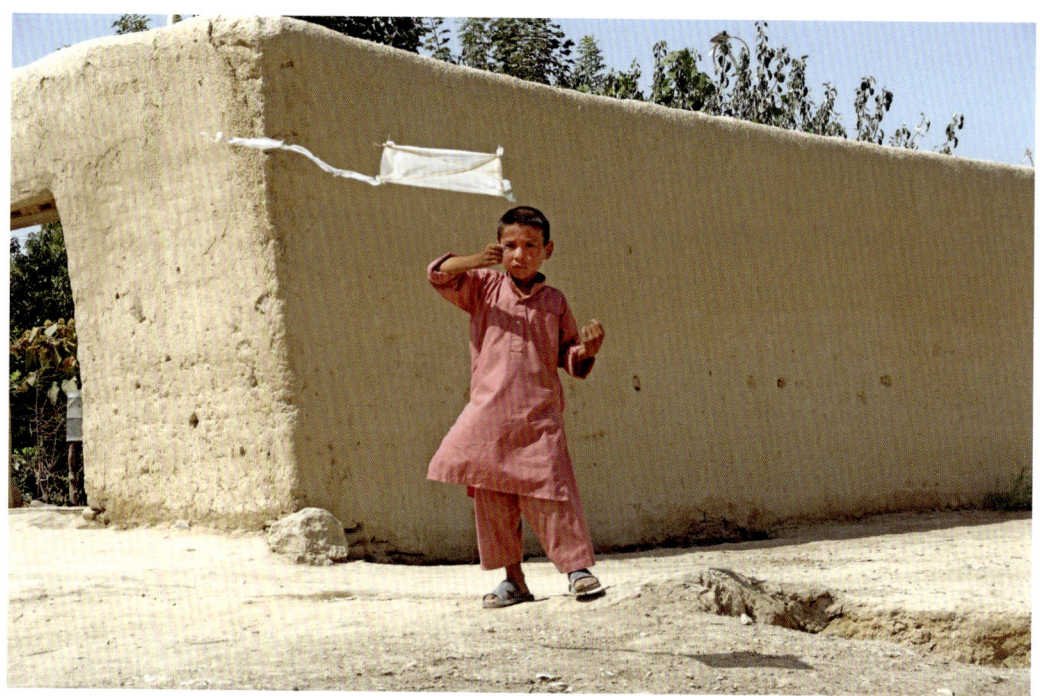

Francis Alÿs, *Children's Game #10: Papalote*, Balkh, Afghanistan, 2011 (still)

Despite socio-political rules within and surrounding the games, the children emerge in public space in togetherness. The interpretation of play as a basic human need that is universal also has a political and social component. Already in the eighteenth century, the philosopher Friedrich Schiller wrote about what makes us human, introducing his concept of the human "play drive" (*Spieltrieb*). In his reasoning, Schiller defines the human condition by categorizing different "drives." "The *sense drive* demands that there shall be change and that time shall have a content; the *form drive* demands that time shall be annulled and that there shall be no change. That drive, therefore, in which both others work in concert is the *play drive*, reconciling becoming with absolute being and change with identity."[9] In other words, Schiller's definition of human nature is based on the idea that play drives us towards action by creating encounters between reason and feeling. Play is where a border is crossed between the need for stability and the urge for change, which relates to our need for freedom, mental and physical. As we see in the *Games*, the children's drive to play guides them towards new social connections despite the boundaries of the contexts they live in. They shape their own communities, create their own politics and their own poetry. They show us how liminal spaces around borders have the potential to be political, communal, social or, in other words, to be spaces of freedom. For instance, in *Children's Game #16: Hopscotch* (2016), filmed in the Sharya Refugee Camp in Iraq, we see clearly how children create their own breathing space through playing hopscotch in big groups, even within such a dire situation of identitary oppression.

Children's Games also shows the importance of reclaiming public space to create this potential for encounter across borders. A concrete example of this, is how the artist made all videos freely available on his website. He thinks they should belong to the public domain, because the games that are played do, too. On another level, Alÿs vanishes from the foreground in the works and simply records children playing, leaving

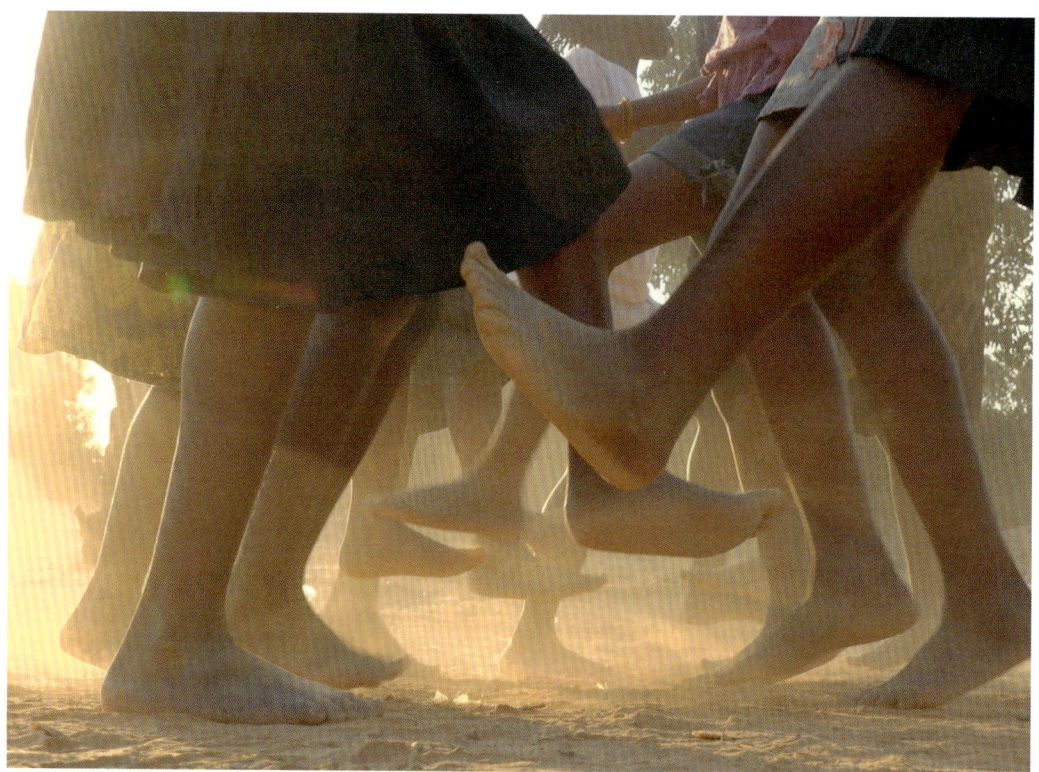

Francis Alÿs, *Children's Game #28: Nzango*, Tabacongo, Democratic Republic of the Congo, 2021 (still)

their space within the public space intact. Many of the games have existed for centuries and are cross-cultural, such as marble games, hopscotch, or musical chairs. The focus in each video lies on the game that is played and the children who can reclaim their own agency to perform without feeling conscious about being recorded. Most children clearly forget the presence of the camera during their moment of play. They share a private moment within their own community, create a temporal universe of their own without shutting it off completely for onlookers or other children who would like to join. By keeping to himself, Alÿs stays in his personal zone and becomes a bystander. This registration of the demarcation lines and tensions between the private and the public space becomes even more explicit in the videos made during the COVID-19 pandemic. Alÿs travelled to Hong Kong, where – after a compulsory quarantine period of two weeks – he looked for children who would meet at the limits of their remaining spaces for play. In *Children's Game #22: Jump Rope* (2020), three girls are playing together but individually, outside in open air but within their private bubble. In a time when being together was politicized and problematized, the space for play these girls created together despite sanitary borders becomes a space for freedom.

IV

Alÿs visits places where children manage to encounter each other in relative harmony, within their own confined worlds of imagination. The games are not a form of escapism from reality, as they take place within its heart, under the public eye. The games become a necessity for a community of children who react and counteract, while finding their own space for freedom and imagination. *Children's Games* is a place of encounter, where the elements that make up a community, such as play, are shown in the children's own reality and imaginary realm. Rather than seeing naïve visions of a world without borders – something very much associated with misleadingly optimistic stories of globalization and multiculturality – I'd like to see the ways in which we can engage each other despite borders, within the potentiality of the liminal space that is created there. As the artist writes it down himself in his note-book: "boundaries are legal fictions / border barriers to /- keep apart / - contain."[10] Crossing a border is necessary to create encounters, and it can very well be regarded a social and political fact. The collection of these children's games will grow, as will the imagination to join them in a collective and playful resistance.

Notes

1. For an overview of Francis Alÿs's oeuvre in these contexts, see for instance: Museo de Arte Moderno (1997). *Francis Alÿs: Walks/Paseos.* Guadalajara: Universidad de Guadalajara; Russell Ferguson, Cuauhtémoc Medina & Jean Fisher (eds.) (2007, revised in 2022). *Francis Alÿs.* London: Phaidon; Mark Godfrey, Klaus Biesenbach, and Kerryn Greenberg (eds.) (2010). *Francis Alÿs: A Story of Deception.* London: Tate Publishing.

2. There are of course exceptions to this repetitive discourse about the work of Francis Alÿs. See, for instance, the essays by Nicole Schweizer and Julia Bryan-Wilson in the 2021 catalogue of the exhibition *Francis Alÿs. As Long As I'm Walking* at the Musée Cantonal des Beaux-Arts, Lausanne, Switzerland (October 15, 2021 – January 16, 2022); N. Schweizer (ed.) (2021). *Francis Alÿs. As Long as I'm Walking.* Geneva: JRP Editions.

3. See Francis Alÿs (2007). *Francis Alÿs: Sometimes doing something poetic can become political and sometimes doing something political can become poetic.* New York: David Zwirner Books.

4. Mark Godfrey (2010). "Politiek/Poëzie: het werk van Francis Alÿs." In *Francis Alÿs: A Story of Deception.* Op. cit., 32.

5. Arjun Appadurai (2000). "Grassroots Globalization and the Research Imagination." *Public Culture* 12/1. 5.

6. I refer hereby to the groundbreaking work of Gloria Anzaldua, who not only aptly describes the complexities of Mexican identity living in the physical borderlands between the US and Mexico – an area which is very relevant to the work of Alÿs – but also explains the psychological, sexual, and spiritual borderlands that abide in a multifarious identity. She explains the pain and the beauty of being so multiple through poetry and acknowledges the intergenerational trauma of colonization by using the languages that assert her and her community's layered identity. Gloria Anzaldua (1987). *Borderlands/La Frontera. The New Mestiza.* San Francisco: Aunt Lute Book Company.

7. Francis Alÿs (2021). "Don't Cross the Bridge Before You Get to the River." David Zwirner website. Retrieved April 20, 2023 from https://www.davidzwirner.com/exhibitions/2021/francis-alys-dont-cross-the-bridge-before-you-get-to-the-river.

8. 59th Biennale di Venezia (2022). *Francis Alÿs: The Nature of the Game.* Berlin: DCV Verlag.

9. Friedrich Schiller (1993). "Letters Upon the Aesthetic Education of Man." *Essays.* Trans. by Elizabeth M. Wilkinson & L.A. Willoughby. London: Bloomsbury Academic. 126.

10. 59th Biennale di Venezia (2022). *Francis Alÿs: The Nature of the Game.* Op. cit.

Entering the Game

Virginia Roy*

One tale is good till another is told.
— Francis Alÿs

I

A hand on top of a hand, and then another, and one more ... until a stack of hands is built. Suddenly, the bottom hand, the one that had been placed first, is placed on top of all of them again, and then the next one ... faster and faster. And even faster. Until creating a dance of hands. The children laugh, pull their hands out and clap their hands with one another, and can no longer manage to put them back in place without hitting each other. *Hand Stack.*

Elsewhere, some girls dance; they are laughing too. We see how their legs follow one another, imitating each other, in a chain of contagious rhythm and movement. *Nzango*, a game that originated in the Democratic Republic of the Congo, becomes a mixture of chants and choreographies. From the very first moment, the energy of these bodies and the liveliness of their voices and laughter hypnotize us and immerse us in their own world.

* Virginia Roy is a curator at MUAC-UNAM (Museo Universitario Arte Contemporáneo, Universidad Nacional Autónoma de México). She co-curated the exhibition *Francis Alÿs. Juegos de niñxs. Children's Games 1999–2022*, which ran from February 11 until September 17, 2023.

II

Francis Alÿs has been collecting children's games from around the world for over twenty years. His series *Children's Games* records different games in which children interact with their peers: musical chairs, hopscotch, rock – paper – scissors, knucklebones ... Myriad children's amusements in the public space document the dynamics of childhood in the street without the intermediation or artifice of the toy. As Alÿs has pointed out, "this compilation favors games that can be made out of nothing, which means that they can be played with anything that can be found where the game will take place, be it a handkerchief, a bit of rope, an empty can... They often are about invention and about adapting the context to the end of the game."[1]

The project gathers together recreational activities carried out in different countries (Democratic Republic of the Congo, Iraq, Venezuela, Belgium, Hong Kong, Mexico, France, Afghanistan, and many more) and shows both the universality of most of the games and the specificity of the societies and cultures where they are inscribed. A dialog is thus created that transcends geographical borders and delves into the ludic as a common space. As an anthropological archive, the series brings together various games that take place in the public space, in an attempt to preserve this cultural heritage in progressive extinction. Passed down for generations, these games are coming to end. The gradual disappearance of public spaces, together with the increasing insecurity and the growing use of technology and video games in childhood, is causing children to play less and less in the street. Even intermediate, semi-public spaces are emerging, such as rooftops or condominiums, which are places for meeting and playful coexistence but not accessible to everyone. This is the case in *Children's Game #22: Jump Rope* (2020). Three girls jump rope on a rooftop in the urbanized megalopolis of Hong Kong. Their skill and speed are admirable.

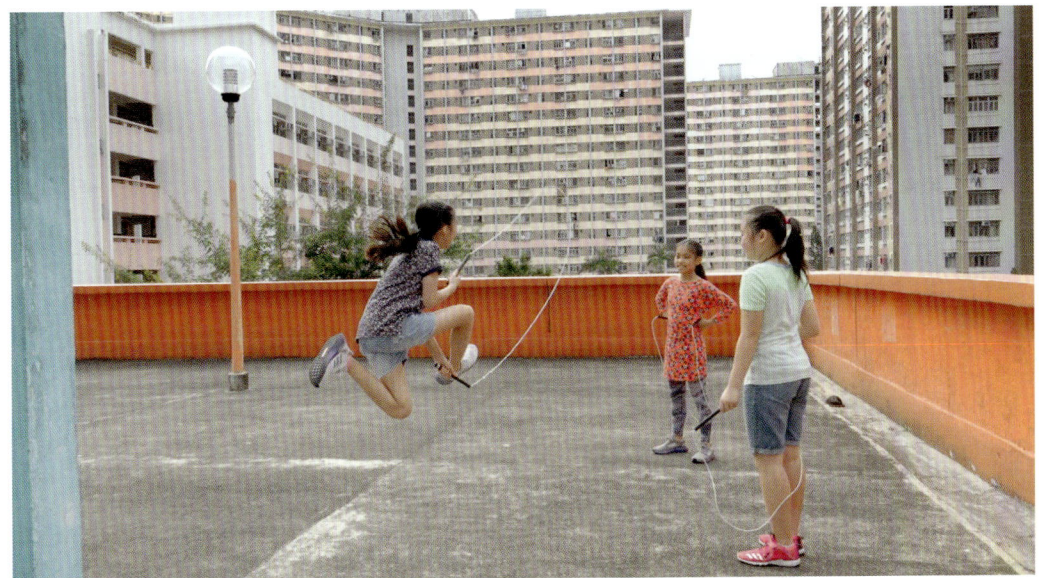

Francis Alÿs, *Children's Game #22: Jump Rope*, Hong Kong, 2020 (still)

The *Children's Games* contain several of the strategies of Alÿs's artistic work: the game, the public space, the drift, the act of collecting, the boundary, the arbitrary, and the effort, including collaboration with children, among others. They are themes that are reflected in Alÿs's previous works, but which in this series take on a specific relevance. The viewer, initially an intruder, is invited to inhabit this playing field that extends beyond the images. Little by little, almost without knowing it, they end up becoming another player who, from the shadows, silently joins in the observation. The pieces thus develop an empathy with the viewer: they allow us to put ourselves in their place, to meet others. They make it possible for us to imagine and connect with the realities and stories we are observing. They bring us closer to the narrative that unfolds in the game. We are challenged, and that sensibility permeates the screen, in a sort of game texture that captivates and moves us. One finds oneself referring back to the memory of one's own childhood or that of one's children, creating layers that overlap times and memories. What did we call that game? (And here almost a dictionary of possibilities and contradictions unfolds). Where did we play it? With whom? And so on and so forth.

This identification becomes an emotional display that evolves like the games themselves and becomes more complex in the pieces: from the contagious freshness and joy we move on to the drama and violence of some social realities where the game is played. Yet we always establish this ability to associate ourselves with what we see and feel, with the other worlds that expand from the image. As Martha Nussbaum has noted, "empathy is a very important tool in the service of getting a sense of what is going on in the other person, and also of establishing concern and connection."[2]

The games are therefore presented as a proposal for permanent relocation, the displacement of oneself in order to relocate in another position. In this process, abstraction takes place on two levels: on the one hand, in the sphere of the game itself, where the child leaves her circumstances *to enter the game* and become a player; on the other hand, at the level of the spectator, who also immerses in this abstraction to enter into the dynamics they contemplate: *to be in the game*. This exercise of empathy reconstructs the experience in the player's mind and leads them to recognize the other and their reality. A game emerges from the image and at the same time the game expands and opens up in the very experience of the exhibition.

This series is not the only one by Francis Alÿs that uses empathy as an aesthetic approach. In fact, most of his pieces operate in this way. Still, it can be highlighted as a relevant process that emerges in the *Children's Games* series. This generated empathy becomes an equalizing procedure, where we all enter the game to participate in the same way. "Films are more about the invisible than the visible, for they provide a channel to the full gamut of human experience: to people's thoughts, emotions, values, and beliefs."[3] In fact, the relevance of emotions as a political platform can already be seen in childhood: "emotions are needed to provide the developing child with a map of the world. … Fear and joy and love and even anger demarcate the world, and at the same time map the self in the world."[4] In this location, the game is a basic instrument for the development of the subjects. In this sense, it is essential to highlight the political dimension of emotions. The current philosophical trend of what has been called the *affective turn*,[5] with authors such as Sarah Ahmed, underscores the importance of affective expressions and their place in cultural and social life. Emotions play a crucial role in the construction of community and in the shaping of a collective imaginary, as well as in the effect of their circulation and contact.

III

Children's Games brings together different games that emphasize gestures and bodily presence. Beyond oral entertainment based on sayings or riddles, in which language plays a structuring role, Alÿs chooses to document games where language does not constitute a boundary. The emphasis lies on communication over words and speech, on the action that takes place, and on its performativity. In Alÿs's opinion, "[w]hereas adults are more likely to use speech to process experiences, children play to assimilate the realities they encounter. Their games mimic, mock or defy the rules of the adult society that surrounds them. The act of playing may also help them coping with traumatic experiences such as those of war by creating a simulacrum of the real and turning the dramatic circumstances around them into a more fictional, ludic world."[6]

The game becomes an autonomous space and its meaning takes on its own unique dimension; it is governed and understood by itself. In this regard, Roger Caillois indicated that "the game has no other but an intrinsic meaning."[7] To this we could add that it is precisely this limitation, this *having no other but*, that grants it its potency and conditions of possibility. The bubble that makes up the game contains its own consciousness and nature of truth. Going back to Caillois, there are several characteristics that the French sociologist stipulated to define play, and which help us to understand the ontological limits of ludic activity:

    1. *Free*: in which playing is not obligatory; if it were, it would at once lose its attractive and joyous quality as diversion;
    2. *Separate*: circumscribed with limits of space and time, defined and fixed in advance;
    3. *Uncertain*: the course of which cannot be determined, nor the result attained beforehand, and some latitude of innovations being left to the player's initiative;

4. *Unproductive*: creating neither goods, nor wealth, nor new elements of any kind; and, except for the exchange of property among the players, ending in a situation identical to the prevailing at the beginning of the game;

5. *Governed by rules*: under conventions that suspend ordinary laws, and for the moment establish new legislation, which alone counts;

6. *Make-believe*: accompanied by a special awareness of a second reality or of a free unreality, as against real life.[8]

Caillois's categories are revealing in terms of the boundaries that operate in the very definition of the game. The activity must be configured as a system that involves rules and takes place in a defined space and time; its outcome becomes unpredictable, and its nature is not to produce anything, not to be utilitarian or lacking in material interest. As we all know, after playing, we go back to the starting point. And we start again, if there is a beginning and an end in the game. As Julio Cortázar said, "nothing more rigorous than a game; children respect the laws of the kite or the little corners with a dedication that they do not put into those of grammar."[9] Indeed, children have an absolute commitment and a total dedication to the game.

As external observers, it is sometimes difficult to decipher the rules, but the actions and disposition of the players convey the credibility of the activity; that is, the rigor and seriousness of their actions. From the inside, the participants have a clear idea of what and what not to do. They respect and follow the rules with a conviction derived from a previous pact, negotiated, self-regulating. In *Children's Game #19: Haram Football* (2017), Alÿs portrays the imaginary football played by children in Mosul, Iraq, during the occupation by the Islamic State. As it was forbidden by the regime, this action became a strategy to circumvent the censorship, an incredible exercise of imagination and consensus among the players. The result is a poetic and heart-rending story that reproduces the ability to agree and the power of creativity and invention.

The freedom and flexibility inherent in the game exist within assumed rules and structure. As Gadamer has pointed out: "The attraction that the game exercises on the player lies in this risk. One enjoys a freedom of decision which at the same time is endangered and irrevocably limited."[10] Taking the game to the limit would imply, as Gilles Deleuze writes, an *ideal* game "without rules, with neither winner or loser": a game that can only be "thought" and fully affirms "chance."[11]

How far does the independence of the game go? One of the successes of Alÿs's project is precisely to address the fissures of this autonomy and explore its tensions with the social, historical, and cultural spaces where the actions are inscribed. He manages to show how the reality of society permeates through the game. Despite the fact that playing is considered an isolated bubble, social issues inevitably penetrate childhood by way of children's amusements. Thus, we see them, for example, in the gender games or in the entertainments that capture the violence and daily reality that children live. Filmed in Ciudad Juárez, a border city between Mexico and the United States, *Children's Game #15: Espejos* (2013) presents some youngsters playing with the gleam of mirrors. Taking cover in uninhabited public housing, they hide and chase each other, trying to avoid the gleam of their opponent's mirror: if the light hits them, they die.

Another fundamental element in the logic of the game is time. In the ludic activity, the notion of time is suspended. The course of reality is paused, and we enter into a time of our own. Time stops, is dilated, is disrupted. The notion of time is lost while playing, and we are introduced in a new temporality, a spiral sequence. The action repeats and repeats,[12] assuming the game's unboundedness, its infinity. Time acquires a new meaning insofar as it is in the game. The same activity can be interrupted at any time and restarted in the same way. This idea is beautifully reflected in *Children's Game #6: Sandcastles* (2009). Three children build sandcastles on the seacoast of Knokke-Le-Zoute in Belgium. What could be considered a foretold failure, as the sea will inevitably bring the castles down, is a challenge for the children as they fight every second of the game in an unequal struggle against the water. Another idea of continuity emerges. Cuauhtémoc Medina points out in this regard:

> Stories and games often lead us to a time before their beginning or force us to start before the place of our departure, defying the convention of the linearity of time that seems to define the ethos of the adult world. Playing a game includes falling back in time and space, regressing and restarting, and suddenly jumping forward and backward, in an enjoyment of the defiance of logic and productivity.[13]

Decidedly, the game re-tells the story.

The children have fun and laugh. They inhabit a tension between the order and structure of rules, as well as the excitement and uncertainty of the game in its own time. *Children's Game #29: La roue* (2021) is set in a cobalt mine in the town of Lubumbashi in the Democratic Republic of the Congo. A boy, with the help of his companions, stoically climbs the mountain by pushing a wheel. The reference to the myth of Sisyphus is evident. We are overwhelmed by the size and scale of the little boy in the landscape. Once at the top, the boy slips inside the wheel and rolls down the mountain. Thrilled by the speed, he smiles with pride at his skill and effort. And he climbs back up again ...

IV

Much has been written about the political and social impacts of laughter. Since ancient times, laughter has been studied and used as a satirical device in society, as well as a comic and mocking mechanism. Yet beyond a social historiography of laughter, I am interested in expounding on Judith Butler's idea of laughter as political rupture. Butler analyzes laughter as a borderline moment of the body, where the body is liberated and opened. The act of laughing is an involuntary emission of sound, an irrational, impulsive noise that breaks the traditional mechanism of communication. "The laughter takes us to the edge of language itself [...] something cannot be transported in its entirety into speech."[14]

Laughter in general is inherent to games, to children's fun, and we observe this in *Children's Games*. What, though, is the significance of that laughter? What is the critical potency of that uproar, and what does it reveal and manifest? As Butler has noted, "there are other forms of political expression that do not conform to speech [...] the sounds of the body exceed the form of vocalization called speech."[15] In the same way that the game is a suspension of time and sense of reality, laughter appears as a rupture of functioning and as a response of the body. The overflow the game represents is reflected in the act of laughing. It is not a deliberate performance; it is a reaction to a situation. Laughter escapes from control. It bursts out. It bursts into everyday life, spontaneously, and becomes a political expression.

The game is fun and laughter, revealing its own communication that expands to the spectator. Laughter has contagious effects and "our intense capacity to be affected by an another involuntary cannot be contained."[16] So, when we look at Alÿs's videos, we find ourselves laughing with the little ones, feeling excited about their achievements. Finally, the snails reach the race line (*Children's Game #31: Slakken* (2021)), or the little runner who had escaped is finally captured (*Children's Game #25: Contagio* (2021)).

It tends to be a shared, expanded and contagious laughter. It is also present in *Children's Game #33: Schneespiele* (2022). A dozen of children entertain themselves in the snowy forests of Switzerland, throwing

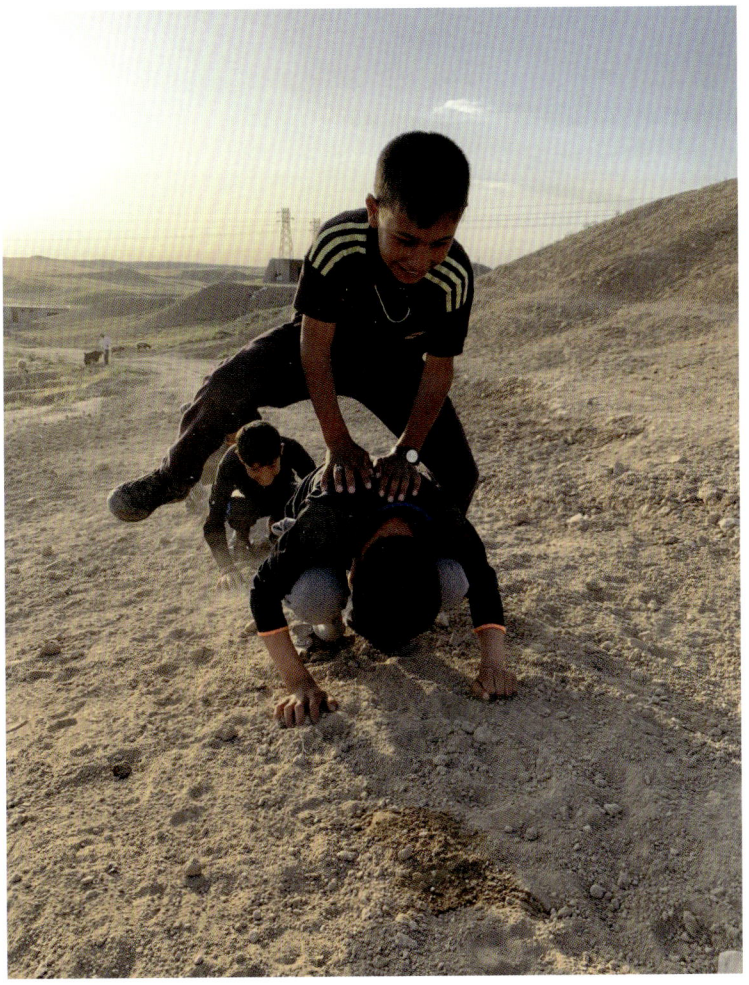

Making of Francis Alÿs, *Children's Game #20: Leapfrog*, Nerkzlia, Iraq, 2018 (photo by the artist)

snowballs and sliding down the hills, but, above all, they laugh. In Denmark, in *Children's Game #34: Appelsindans* (2022), several children play in pairs. Each couple holds an orange with their foreheads, and when they become unbalanced and the orange falls to the ground, they lose. Yet they always laugh. Another example is the well-known game of leapfrog. We are in Afghanistan, *Children's Game #20: Leapfrog* (2018). In a long line, several children jump over each other in laughter. All share in the merriment: those who jump, those who are jumped, and those who watch. Movements, glances, and noise fascinate and seduce.

Laughing, then, becomes an affirmation and an enunciation of the game, as well as the manifestation and expression of a sociability. Laughter allows us, according to Butler, to "inhale life-giving breath from the others,"[17] to perceive solidarity. Situated on the edge of language, "laughter wills the power of renewal, it's a kind of contagion with the shaking of the body that forms the bonds of community."[18] The appearance of children and their smiles is an affirmation of them as political subjects, as participants in the public sphere. There is power in laughter, and a space of that which is imaginary and, at the same time, possible. In the magic and texture of the game, we are associated with the world, as well as with others.

Notes

1. Francis Alÿs (2023). *Exhibition text for Francis Alÿs. Juegos de niñxs. Children's Games 1999–2022*, MUAC-UNAM.

2. Martha C. Nussbaum (2001). *Upheavals of thought. The Intelligence of Emotions.* Cambridge: Cambridge University Press. 330–331.

3. David MacDougall, "Francis Alÿs and the Games of Childhood." In 59th Biennale di Venezia (2022). *Francis Alÿs: The Nature of the Game.* Berlin: DCV Verlag.

4. Martha C. Nussbaum (2001). Op. cit., 206–207.

5. Although previous authors have referred to the importance of emotions in the public sphere, the term was finally coined by Patricia Ticineto Clough and Jean Halley (eds.) (2007). *The Affective Turn.* Durham: Duke University Press.

6. Francis Alÿs (2023). Op. cit.

7. Roger Caillois (2001). *Man, Play and Games.* Trans. Meyer Barash. Urbana, IL: University of Illinois Press. 7. The idea of the game as unproductive, as pure expenditure is linked to Georges Bataille's concept of *depénse*, as Luis Pérez Oramas (2023) has pointed out: "What happens in them means nothing other than what happens there," in "Francis Alÿs and Children's Games: The Helicopter and the Grasshoper." In *Francis Alÿs, Children's Games.* Exhibition catalog Museo Universitario Arte Contemporáneo. Mexico. 71. Retrieved May 5 from https://muac.unam.mx/assets/docs/folio_muac_099_francis_alys.pdf.

8. Roger Caillois (2001). Op. cit., 9–10.

9. Julio Cortázar (1969). *Último Round* [Last Round]. Mexico: Siglo XXI Editores. 66. Author's translation: "Nada más riguroso que un juego; los niños respetan las leyes del barrilete o las esquinitas con un ahínco que no ponen en las de la gramática."

10. Hans-Georg Gadamer (1994). *Truth and Method*. Trans. Joel Weinsheimer and Donald G. Marshall. New York: Continuum. 106.

11. Gilles Deleuze (1990). *The Logic of Sense*. Trans. Mark Lester & Charles Stivale. New York: Columbia University Press. 60.

12. Repetition is another artistic strategy in Francis Alÿs's work.

13. Cuauhtémoc Medina (2019). "A Collection of 'Innumerable Little Allegories.'" In *Francis Alÿs, Children's Games*. Amsterdam: Eye Museum. 15.

14. Judith Butler, "Out of Breath: Laughing, Crying at the Body's Limit." Lecture given at Sala Nezahualcóyotl, Centro Cultural Universitario, UNAM. June 13, 2019.

15. Ibid.

16. Ibid.

17. Ibid.

18. Ibid.

The Right to Play

Juan Martín Pérez García*

(Translated from the Spanish by Miguel González Virgen)

I

Those who are familiar with Francis Alÿs's aesthetic approach to children's games will agree with me that it is engaging, fun, and thoughtful. This is the case whether one watches his videos on his website, turns the pages of his printed books, and even more when one goes through the experience of contemplating the exhibition in a museum. On viewing the exhibition at the University Museum of Contemporary Art of the National Autonomous University of Mexico (MUAC-UNAM), the first element that comes to mind is the recovery of the aesthetic dimension of the everyday game. The close-ups and cuts in the flow of each of the videos engage our eyes in a constant displacement between our adult sight and the gaze of the children who are playing on screen. Inevitably, we are led back to our own memories of joy when we were children. Yet we are also led to remember the different games we played back then, and, especially, to experience anew the playful laughs and cheers of other children. The games originate in different times and different countries which have, somehow, become familiar to us. Through the visual experience of other children's games, the work of Alÿs prompts each of us to be playful again and to rediscover that all boys and girls, no matter their original culture, play freely and with lots of fun while they turn any object into a work of art and play.

* Juan Martín Pérez García is the Executive Director of the Network for the Rights of Children in Mexico (REDIM) and Executive Secretary of the Latin American and Caribbean Network for the Defense of Children and Adolescents. He was a visitor of *Francis Alÿs. Juegos de niñxs. Children's Games 1999–2022*, presented at MUAC-UNAM (Museo Universitario Arte Contemporáneo, Universidad Nacional Autónoma de México) from February 11 until September 17, 2023.

In the case of Alÿs's *Children's Games*, experiencing the videos in an art space adds to the pleasure. You will find lots of laughter, fun, and movement. The exhibition rooms are left in a semi-darkness that makes for a kind of individual anonymity which, in turn, prevents the adult attitude to get in the way of playfully moving around the video screens or sitting on the rolling stools. I watched and enjoyed the exhibition next to other people I did not know. I shared with them the pleasure of being in the middle of children's games and of laughter that mixed with our own.

II

Do you remember the last time you were playing carefree with other children? Do you feel embarrassment, fear, or anxiety when you imagine yourself now, a fully adult person, who plays children's games? Alÿs's work is a wonderful tool that can help us identify what I call our own adult-centrism, that is, the self-imposed paradigm by which we consider normal and even desirable the inequality of children and young people in relation to us adults. In this paradigm *they* are deemed inferior, incapable, and the private property of families. Alÿs's work enables each of us to examine our own past relation with games and, through that, to trace our passage from children to adults and from there to 'successful' individuals. Most of us get to play freely as children yet within the boundaries set by our family, by the school where we study, and by the community in which we live. Until we become teenagers. At this point, we are pressured by an adult-centric culture to become grown-ups and thereby leave behind childish games. It is the moment when we are ushered into accepting the rigidity of the adult world, now understood as a sphere of seriousness. And we are made to accept gender roles based on unequal power relations.

Games are usually considered childish to diminish their importance in relation to the 'serious adult issues.' We forget that playing is one of the most important elements of everyday life, something of extreme and vital relevance for our own metabolic and cognitive development. In the past years academic research in psychology and, even more recently, the neurosciences has shown that active games that involve running, jumping, and pulling or pushing have a significant impact on the metabolic development of children.[1] These activities improve cardiovascular and lung capacity and contribute to weight control by reducing the levels of fat in the body. Sports medicine has shown that constant physical activity in the early years of life can have a positive effect on a child's mental health, reducing stress and improving their sense of well-being. In addition, neuroscience research has shown that children who participate in moderate to vigorous physical activity perform better on cognitive tests than children who do not, since this activity stimulates the growth of new brain cells and improves neuronal connectivity, a process known as neuroplasticity. This capacity for change is particularly strong in childhood and adolescence when the brain is in constant development. For this reason, during these years, games can improve the activities and plasticity of the prefrontal cortex, a region of the brain involved in focusing attention, reasoning, making decisions, and controlling emotions – functions that are critical for learning and cognitive development. This scientific research is part of the background for the urgent call made by the World Health Organization (WHO) to follow up on the consequences of the second, post-COVID-19 pandemic.[2] The prolonged confinement, sedentary way of life, and the intense exposure to digital screens during the first pandemic had put the issue of our children's mental well-being high on its agenda.

Research in the neurosciences suggests that free play, that is, play without the interference of adults, helps children develop social and emotional skills such as empathy, cooperation, and autonomy.[3] When playing among equals, children have the opportunity to interact with other persons' perspectives and interests on equal terms. This interaction in turn leads them to learn crucial social skills like conflict resolution, negotiation, communication, and teamwork. Games can also help them to develop the capacity to recognize their own emotions and those of others, something that is fundamental to the development of empathy. Through games, children learn to understand the feelings and points of view of the others, something that will guide them towards building solid and meaningful relationships with their friends. When children play freely, they acquire emotional skills like patience, perseverance, and impulse control by learning to wait for their turn, to accept defeat, and to celebrate the victory of somebody else. Taken together, these skills help the children to develop the capacity to manage frustration and anxiety. There is growing evidence that team play has a positive impact on children by allowing them to incorporate into their mental processes decision-making, planning, the search for alternatives, the ability to accept help from others, and a sense of progressive autonomy. Through the acts of cooperation involved in team play children learn to value the contribution made by each member of the group, in addition to acknowledging that in the diversity of every person resides a unique set of skills and strengths.

In Alÿs's *Children's Games* we find confirmation of the importance of free play: all the games he has selected are played without the direct supervision of adults. Their aesthetic beauty allows us to understand the great damage we can cause when we try to hinder the free play among equals, especially in the case of teenagers who are under the pressure to behave like 'young men or young women.' By trying to guide a game into what we adults want, we end up inhibiting the potential of the game to assist in the free development of the personality of both children and teenagers.

When it comes to playing, the adult-centric worldview places children and adults in unequal roles with very different objectives: in our role as adults, we usually emphasize the educational value of a game over its funny, free, and spontaneous qualities. The contents and the rules of games are very often defined through adult surveillance, which reduces the game to a grown-up's definition of enjoyment. Reflect back on the last children's party you attended, and perhaps you will remember two particular moments: on the one hand, those moments you had to play the part in adult rituals and were required to keep up appearances vis-à-vis the other participants; and, in contrast to this scripted scene, the free and noisy play of all the children who were in a totally separate space, different from that of the adults.

III

On account of the positive, metabolic, and cognitive impact of free play, it has been defined as a human right, closely associated with other human rights such as education, health, and voluntary participation. Through games, children can learn to make their own decisions, to express their own interests, and to develop a sense of progressive autonomy. Since 1989, these skills have been defined by the Convention on the Rights of Children (CRC) of the United Nations, which in Article 31 of its final resolution states that "States Parties recognize the right of the child to rest and leisure, to engage in play and recreational activities appropriate to the age of the child and to participate freely in cultural life and the arts."[4] This international treaty establishes twenty interdependent children's rights, grouped under child prevention, provision, protection, and participation. Signatory states are the guarantors of the human rights of children along with their families, who have a shared responsibility for their application, their use, and their accountability.

As a result, adults must shift away from the old paradigm that considers children as 'objects to be protected' to acknowledge children as 'subjects with rights,' as citizens. This shift brings a new dimension to the parental responsibility that, exercised with care and affection, must move towards an educational accompaniment that enables children to exercise their full rights. Ultimately, it is a question of us becoming a positive influence in their life project.

IV

We know that when a girl is born, gender designation will have an important impact on her life. From that moment on, a macho culture can assign her specific gender roles that are continuously reinforced by the family, school, and community environments.[5] Clothing, physical gestures, narratives, and games will all be essential tools for molding her into a 'good girl.' Young girls are blocked from playing many games due to uncomfortable skirts. Similarly, the imposed definition of femininity and the hypersexualization of many games lead young girls to specific forms of play which are actually 'empty signifiers' that can then be filled by the macho gaze with its own desires. Feminist research has examined how games and toys also work towards reinforcing traditional gender roles for girls, especially through dolls, small domestic objects, and simulated make-believe. By way of contrast, boys are made to play games that involve violence, competition, and strength.

For *Children's Games* Alÿs made a very balanced selection of gender-neutral games while also including games where only girls play. For example, *Children's Game #4: Elastic* (2008) is a game that has historically been assigned to girls while boys have been denied the possibility of playing it, because 'playing like a girl' can be used as macho aggression against them. This feature means that many socially imposed games reproduce the hegemonic culture that children assimilate when they play. However, free play can have an opposite effect, allowing children to liberate themselves, at least momentarily, from the social pressure that comes from the adults. When playing freely, children frequently organize their games in a horizontal manner, without gender stereotypes and with social roles based on cooperation. They usually do this without stopping to consider each other's gender, (dis)ability, ethnic origin, or economic status. In other words, free play is a means to both prevent and overcome discrimination.

Educating children against macho culture can start with an examination of the games we ask them to play. We would do well to avoid games that assume the stereotypical male/female roles demanded by traditional patterns of upbringing. Free play brings about a fundamental development of the personality of our children and their sense of citizenship. Playing freely, children share information and express their personal opinions while also understanding that they need to listen to each other if they want the fun to go on. Finally, they learn to reorganize themselves continuously in order to maintain the atmosphere of cooperation-without-discrimination that makes the game possible.

V

If children are to exercise the right to engage in play, national states have the duty to create the conditions that allow all children and teenagers to enjoy rest and leisure. This responsibility includes providing public spaces where they can organize games based on group cooperation. Obviously, this right will be severely restricted when streets are privatized for commercial purposes, when cars are deemed more important than children walking, or when public playgrounds are commercial venues. In these instances, opportunities for children's play lose out at the hands of adult interests. Moreover, this adult appropriation of children's spaces leads to a constantly growing condition of segregation. It reproduces discrimination on the basis of poverty levels, skin color, migration status, geographical location, or social conditions. This inequity can even be the case in schools, where the reduction in playground area will negatively impact the socializing processes of children of the same age, identity, and culture. Despite the obstacles that adults may put in place against play, however, the impulse for playing oftentimes leads children to adjust their dynamic and to transform their environment to regroup themselves. Games, in order words, guide children in their evolution towards autonomy, in building identity, and in learning emotional regulation.

Hand in hand with the current agreements to protect basic human rights, all available research points out that educational organizations ought to consider the right to play as an essential element in bringing up children. It entails questioning the adult-centric paradigm and designing playgrounds for children's sizes and easy access. Local playgrounds should be designed with the participation of children, the main users of the area, so that they may include more ergonomic and diverse types of equipment. It is sad to witness how in big cities, where most of the world population lives, public space has been gradually reduced. Open parks are increasingly fenced off, and safe paths leading to schools are disappearing due to commercial, traffic, and real estate priorities. As adults, we need to keep in mind our educational goals, while people in government positions must remember their own legal obligations to respect and protect the public space of children.

VI

In Mexico and Latin America seven out of ten families do not allow their children to go out due to conditions of insecurity. Walking alone to schools, visiting friends, or going to public playgrounds is no longer considered safe for children. Our cities and our communities are now under the risk of being taken over by violence. This vulnerability has severely disrupted access to public spaces for recreation, which have often become no-go areas for children and teenagers. In our countries, adults talk nostalgically about the games of a not-so-distant past, of times when they were able to play in the streets and explore other barrios, of long periods of play with children from the neighborhood – things which now literally belong to the past century. This situation is not an instance of collective paranoia. It is a reality in a region where thousands of victims disappear en masse. In Mexico, more than 112,000 individuals have officially gone missing; of them, 18,000 are children, mostly young girls. In our country, four children and teenagers under the age of seventeen are killed every day. In the wake of the long COVID-19 pandemic confinement, sexual attacks grew by 50 percent in homes, schools, and churches.[6]

Driven by hopelessness, parents are led to believe that they protect their children by keeping them fixed to digital screens. They do this without any intention of damaging their health, but once movement is reduced, a sedentary lifestyle sets in. This behavior brings along changes in eating habits and, consequently, a growing epidemic of obesity: 36 percent of all children in Mexico are now overweight. Without a well-articulated response from the state, its institutions, and its citizens, an urban landscape of empty swings will continue to be the main feature of schools and playgrounds encircled by violence.

Yet even in war children play. In Alÿs's astonishing *Children's Games #19: Haram Football* (2017) all possible confusion about the movement of the ball is overcome. The ball does not exist and thus remains invisible in the video, but we can nonetheless follow it through the camera's many movements and the teenagers' eyes and passing gestures. The video fills us with hope as we watch how a game of group cooperation adapts itself to the circumstances. It preserves the fun, the play of the ball, and maybe also the resistance to armed violence and to the denigration of public space. This game is the highest expression of the complicity that is needed to rework environments of violence.

In Mexico, videos have gone viral of children who play cops and robbers, though with a twist: the robbers are *sicarios* (cartel assassins) or gang members, while the cops are army soldiers. The clothing and movements of the children resemble the uniforms and actions of criminal gangs. Children's parties are being organized with the theme of *la chapiza*, a social media fad launched by a young group of *sicarios* who work for the sons of a notorious former cartel leader. Like Alÿs's *Children's Game #5: Revolver* (2009) and *Children's Game #15: Espejos* (2013), these games reproduce the violence that is lived by children. Perhaps, though, it is their way to come to terms with their own vulnerability in the face of incompetent authorities. For most people in Mexico these games are either controversial, funny, or alarming. Yet few people stop to consider what these children are actually thinking and what the conditions are of the violence that surrounds them. Even less people will consider the duties that we have as adults to ensure that children can live free of violence. We have in front of us an enormous regional challenge. As adults, as members of institutions, we must work to stop widespread armed violence and help games to return to the public space so that, one day, we can again see our children playing the kind of games that Alÿs has documented all over the world.

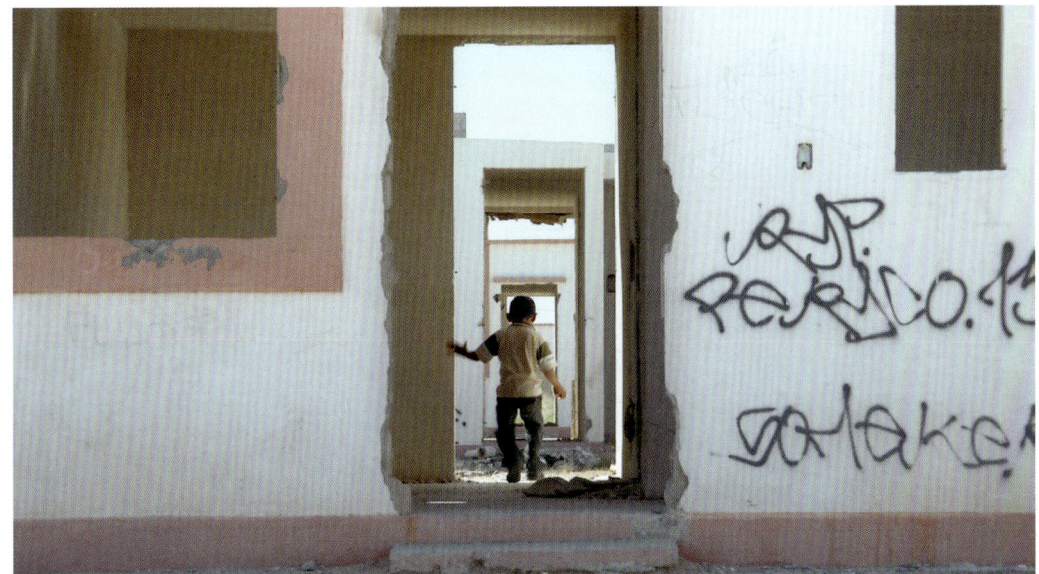

Francis Alÿs, *Children's Game #15: Espejos*, Ciudad Juárez, Mexico, 2013 (still)

Notes

1. Claire Liu, Lynneth Solis, Hanne Jensen, Emily J. Hopkins, Dave Neale, Jennifer M. Zosh, Kathy Hirsh-Pasek & David Whitebread (2017). "Neuroscience and Learning Through Play: A Review of the Evidence." *The Lego Foundation.* DOI:10.13140/RG.2.2.11789.84963; Joe L. Frost (1998). "Neuroscience, Play, and Child Development." Paper presented at the IPA/USA Triennial National Conference. Longmont, CO. June 18–21, 1998. Retrieved May 2, 2023 from https://eric.ed.gov/?id=ED427845.

2. World Health Organization (2023). "A Clinical Case Definition for post COVID-19 condition in Children and Adolescents by Expert Consensus." Retrieved May 1, 2023 from https://www.who.int/publications/i/item/WHO-2019-nCoV-Post-COVID-19-condition-CA-Clinical-case-definition-2023-1 (p. 13); World Health Organization (2022). "Mental Health and COVID-19: Early Evidence of the Pandemic's Impact." Retrieved May 1, 2023 from https://www.who.int/publications/i/item/WHO-2019-nCoV-Sci_Brief-Mental_health-2022.1.

3. Hillary L. Burdette & Robert C. Whitaker (2005). "Resurrecting Free Play in Young Children, Looking Beyond Fitness and Fatness to Attention, Affiliation, and Affect." *Archives of Pediatrics and Adolescent Medicine.* 159/1. 46–50. DOI:10.1001/archpedi.159.1.46 (https://jamanetwork.com/journals/jamapediatrics/article-abstract/485902); Stephen Rushton (2011). "Neuroscience, Early Childhood Education and Play: We are Doing it Right!" *Early Childhood Education Journal.* 39. 89–94. https://doi.org/10.1007/s10643–011-0447-z.

4. United Nations (1989). "Convention on the Rights of the Child." Retrieved May 1, 2023 from https://www.ohchr.org/en/instruments-mechanisms/instruments/convention-rights-child#:~:text=Article%2031,-1.&text=States%20Parties%20recognize%20the%20right,cultural%20life%20and%20the%20arts.

5. Iris Marion Young (1980). "Throwing like a Girl. A Phenomenology of Feminine Body Comportment, Motility and Spatiality." *Human Studies.* 3/2.

6. For a daily updated overview of the numbers of reported missing persons in Mexico, see https://versionpublicarnpdno.segob.gob.mx/Dashboard/Index; see also REDIM - INEGI (2022) for homicide data of children and adolescents in Mexico, https://blog.derechosinfancia.org.mx/2022/03/14/defunciones-por-agresiones-de-infancia-y-adolescencia-en-mexico/.

The Echo of the Children's Games

Hilde Teerlinck*

A young boy runs and falls on the ground while his leg slides over the dirt street and the tip of his foot touches an imaginary ball, and he scores a goal! An action comparable to the likes of Messi! You can feel the joy on the dry and dusty streets. Even if the ball isn't there, he is there.

...

The high notes of the boys entice the mosquitos to circle above their heads, seducing thousands of them to enter the trap that kills them.

...

In a cloud of dust and sand, young girls gracefully dance to the melody of their songs, a battle of barefooted bodies challenging each other.

...

A girl in a school uniform jumps through the busy streets of Hong Kong, trying not to step on a crack, a dangerous game only she is aware of while she whispers the words that drive her through the city.

...

Armed with a small piece of mirror in their hands, these children hide and run through the ruins of uninhabited houses, searching for the others with the seemingly harmless reflection of the sun.

...

* Hilde Teerlinck is a Belgian curator and General Director of the Han Nefkens Foundation, Barcelona. She was the curator of *Francis Alÿs. The Nature of the Game*, presented at the Belgian pavilion during the 59th Venice Biennale from April 23 until November 27, 2022.

Wherever I go, the exhibition of *Children's Games* in Venice still echoes. People were moved by the multi-screen installation that was presented in the Belgian pavilion for the 59th Venice Biennale. The installation at the heart of the pavilion was composed of 14 children's games filmed in different parts of the world. It invited visitors to walk through a labyrinth of projections as if they were standing in the middle of a busy, global playground. The sound and image of the different films interacted with each other – they were fragments forming a whole; allegories translating the complexity of a harsh reality. The whole experience was immersive and intense indeed. Yet why were we so moved? Whatever background or culture we came from, we almost all connected with *The Nature of the Game*. Why?

It is not easy to film children, especially today, when most are so used to moving images. Instagram, Facebook, TikTok, YouTube … Children change their attitude once they notice the camera. Before you know it, you have lost the moment you wanted to capture: their engrossment in the game instead of the camera. It requires a special connection, a predisposition, to take children seriously and to respect the rules of their games.

The rules are not always written, yet they are very clear to those who are playing. When children play, they become completely absorbed in the game. They continue playing, no matter what happens around them. They have the capacity to be completely immersed in it, losing any notion of time. It is this ability to focus that we, as adults, lack. However, it is not only about the ability to focus. It also requires great creativity to create a parallel world, different from the one we might know as sometimes complex and terrifying.

Playing might be a way to escape or to understand the challenging conditions some children live in. Through playing, they survive. Even when it comes to traumatic experiences, children will use their toys,

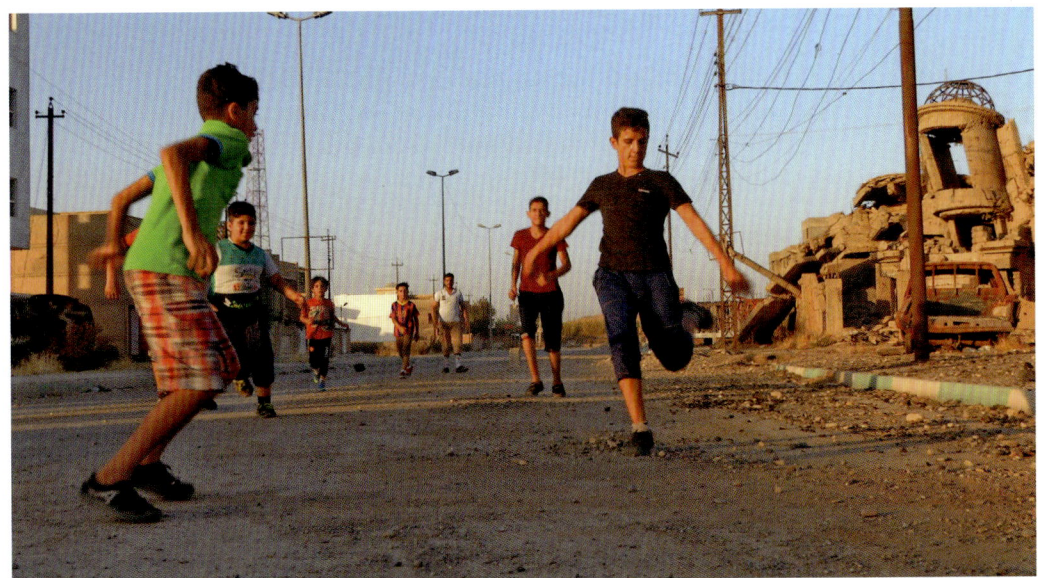

Francis Alÿs, *Children's Game #19: Haram Football*, Mosul, Iraq, 2017 (still)

their bodies, and their games to express, to understand, and to cure where we, as adults, need words.

I still remember the film I saw in the Istanbul Biennial in 2017, *Wonderland* by Erkan Özgen, in which the body language of Mohammed is more powerful than any story, text, or spoken word. There is a direct and immediate connection between what we see and what we feel.

The body language in the films of Alÿs's installation at the Venice Biennale is inestimable. Due to the restriction of in-person meetings during COVID-19, we appear today to be more responsive to body language than ever. We have experienced the poverty of online conversations, the tiring situation of not being able to read the unspoken language in virtual meetings. A conversation means listening with all of our senses; engaging with the other requires feeling the unsaid. We need all of these different inputs to process data.

Did we notice that spoken language is almost absent in the *Children's Games*? Alÿs and his team marvelously capture the subtle moments of moving body parts; eyes and feet that talk, smile, and play; pieces that successfully portray interactions; and exchanges that take place between all actors of the game. They generously give us honesty and seriousness but also humor and joy. Perhaps the necessity to engage with the non-verbal makes it so easy to be emotionally moved by the films.

The game is not only about the protagonists of the game but also about the public, the children surrounding the game. In *Children's Game #27: Rubi* (2021) the crowd is as important for the players as the game itself. The crowd encourages, participates, exchanges with the players. The crowd creates a sense of community. When a chicken invades the playground, they all burst out laughing, but as soon as they can, they return to the game. They create an organic sense of belonging and sharing in space. This feeling is one we definitely all have – and need.

Undeniably, the *Children's Games* are linked to childhood. We have all been a child; we have all played and have grown up since. Could it be the sense of nostalgia that triggers our emotions? As most of the games are universal and have been played for many years, we inevitably recognize them, and they (re)evoke memories of our childhood, memories composed of image, as well as of sound. Sound plays a major role here: the different sounds of each video come together and create a composition. It is a playful and joyful melody. Alÿs searches for a balance that creates a musical landscape that we move through, one that fully engages with our emotions. Perhaps this is also what stimulates the production of dopamine in our brains?

Alÿs also uses his camera as a way to try to understand the culture and the patterns by which people live. He noticed that although some of the games are related to a specific geographical or cultural tradition, most of them are played all over the world, giving them a universal character. Yet it seems more than universal: it seems embedded in our DNA.

Its juxtaposition of the location of the games (Democratic Republic of the Congo, Taiwan, Switzerland, Afghanistan or Mexico) creates a stimulating and inspiring dialog. The locations reinforce each other. Oddly enough, they do not compete with each other; they complete each other. It is a living archive where the films are pieces of an endless puzzle fitting perfectly together.

The games are filmed in different social, cultural, and political societies. Alÿs is often invited to work in and investigate societies in deep conflict. In an extraordinarily earnest way, his works speak about these injustices while using a poetic language. Alÿs does not hide the harsh realities he points out. As he often says, when a situation stops making any sense, it sometimes takes the absurdity of the artistic act to re-introduce a measure of meaning. This situation happens in *Children's Game #29: La roue* (2021), where we can see more than just the tip of the iceberg of the social, economic, and political complexity of the Democratic Republic of the Congo.

I often heard people speaking about the feeling of hope that was present in the *Children's Games* installation. Hope in a little boy of only five years old who pushes a tire nearly as big as himself up a mountain, who gets inside gracefully, and rolls back down the mountain. Hope in the songs he and his friends sing. Hope in the boy with his kite in Afghanistan, playing a sport banned by the Taliban (*Children's Game #10: Papalote* (2011)).

When playing, children naturally cross the borders of contractions in societies they live in, creating a temporary space where they can live fully. They create spaces of freedom.

We thought that COVID-19 would teach us to slow down, to take care of each other, to take time to face our responsibilities in the world, to also enjoy and play. Will the echoes of the *Children's Games* inspire us to change?

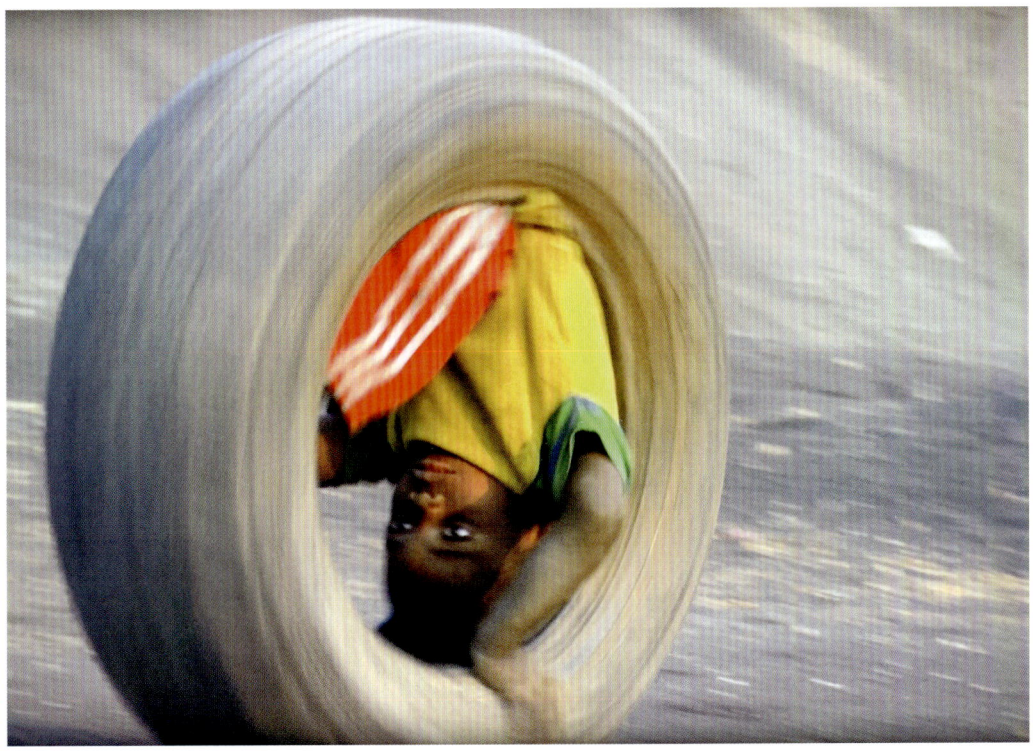

Francis Alÿs, *Children's Game #29: La roue*, Lubumbashi, Democratic Republic of the Congo, 2021 (still)

Curating Connection and Cultural Memory

Reflections on an Encounter with *The Nature of the Game* at the Venice Biennale in 2022

John Potter*

I

Children's games may seem ephemeral, played and then gone. In truth, they are locked in personal and cultural memory, waiting for a trigger to bring them back out into the light of day. In some countries, mine for example (the UK or Ireland), these triggers include snatches of sound from a school, the sight of a playground full of markings, or a child running by in a park, counting, ducking behind a tree, and peering out from a hiding place. In the Belgian pavilion at the Venice Biennale in 2022, Francis Alÿs and the curatorial team produced a series of huge triggers of memory, enticing adults and children alike into monumental, votive video displays of games from many cultures and spaces. Like beautiful, sustained repositories of feelings and ideas, encoded with rules and teetering, sometimes collapsing into chaos, these games were expanded and reframed. They reworked Alÿs's online collection into new light and new life.[1]

* John Potter is Professor of Media in Education at University College London. He visited the exhibition *Francis Alÿs. The Nature of the Game*, presented at the Belgian pavilion during the 59th Venice Biennale from April 23 until November 27, 2022.

One by one, each screen in *The Nature of the Game* drew me in and revealed a children's game from somewhere in the world. They reminded me that these games are both specific and universal. I almost missed them. I was at a conference in Mestre, and, on a free day, I travelled by bus and boat over to the Biennale, into the bright heat of the Giardini and the orchestra of insects in the bushes and trees. I visited a few pavilions and wandered serendipitously through the heat. About to leave, I headed into one final exhibition, in the Belgian pavilion, but then found it very hard to leave. Pausing by the beautiful, intricate, smaller introductory paintings, I was drawn into the main space by an eerie sound: a kind of drone, but produced by voice. It was no synthesis of instruments or guitar-produced noise but a sort of calling or beckoning, shifting slightly in pitch but never straying far from a single note. On the large screen immediately in front of me, in the gathering dusk of a sub-Saharan African country, the sound was emanating from the upturned faces of children. They called down a swarm of insects which descended towards their waiting hands and were then clapped out of existence. This was *Children's Game #30: Imbu* (2021), a game from Tabacongo in the Democratic Republic of the Congo. *Imbu* had a new purpose in this filmed and relocated form, luring the casual visitor from the brightly lit opening into the darkness of the main exhibition space. The video was set up near the entrance and guided us towards further screens alongside and beyond.

In the version on the Alÿs's website, *Imbu* takes its place alongside the catalogued and numbered games that are being collected as short videos since 1999. It has received the number 30, dates from 2021, and runs for 4'58".[2] The difference between the games on the website and the gallery presentations is vast. In the gallery, the flat plane of the laptop screen is expanded and gives way to a beautifully designed three-dimensional space. Many of the games are shown at monumental scale. I use the term 'monumental' deliberately here, not only drawing attention to the size

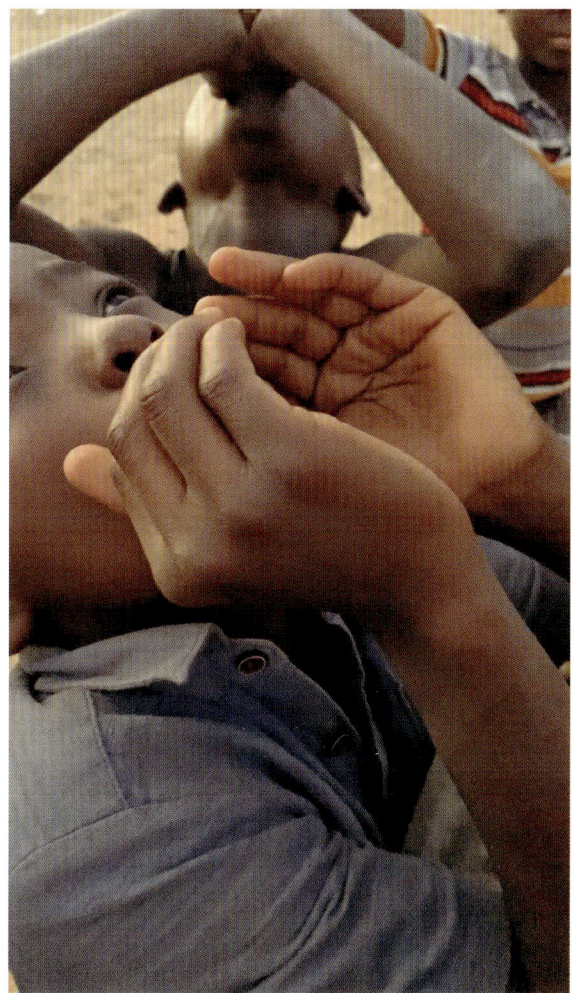

Francis Alÿs, *Children's Game #30: Imbu*, Tabacongo, Democratic Republic of the Congo, 2021 (still)

of the projected images but also to what appears to be the votive space in which they are presented. These videos now hint at meanings larger than mere documentation. We are invited to contemplate children's games as the center of a cultural experience, not as throwaway ephemera. Children's games are relocated from the margins to the center of the stage. And so, too, therefore, are children and even childhood itself. These have now become a site of meaning-making, with their own rule systems and internal logics. In some cases they remain outside societal rule systems and draw on all available resources to refashion experience.

II

The Nature of the Game makes us look at children's games differently. Through carefully filmed and edited video representations – curated, labelled, and presented in a series of screens – the exhibition invites visitors to find their own path through the space. Other artists in Venice achieve this votive display and path within the materiality of popular culture. If we think of Sonia Boyce's brilliant exhibition about Black British soul singers, we see some parallels with Alÿs's project. In the British pavilion, Boyce makes us think about what it means to move Black British soul singers into the center of an exhibition. She focuses on issues of representation, recognition, and remembering in the screenings, the album sleeves, and the newly filmed performances.[3] In the Belgian pavilion, the childhood game has received a similar level of attention, having been moved into a central gallery frame. The commentary is the detail of the game, the time and place, the carefully shot and edited pieces made by Alÿs, his team, and local collaborators.

Gazing on into the space after *Imbu*, the eye is drawn towards two screens. On one of them is a game we think we know about, on the other, a game which looks strange and unfamiliar. The first of these, to the right, is an enthusiastic, dazzling game of jump rope, as seen in many playgrounds and urban spaces. The second, straight ahead, is a looming, human-made mountain and a tiny figure pushing a truck tire. The figure makes its way up a steep, almost impossible slope. This is *Children's Game #29: La roue* (2021). Like *Imbu*, it is a game from the Democratic Republic of the Congo. Before any detail of where and when is absorbed from the information panel, however, skillful filming and editing draw the gallery visitor into the struggle of the climb and, ultimately, its purpose. Its scale is breathtaking, as the camera locates the action via a long shot of the huge, slate grey mountain and the vista beyond, back into the world. The mountain is the mine in reverse, the excavated slag heap of detritus, expelled from the earth, piled, and looming high over the city. In the earliest establishing shots, we see the machinery, the towers, chimney stacks, skeletal metal structures, and corrugated sheets behind the boy as he struggles with the unruly and very heavy tire which is almost as tall as he is. In the near distance is the city of Lubumbashi. As he is joined by three others, about one minute into the video, we see that the children up close are determined, focused, and in control. While there is real work involved in steering the heavy tire up the slope, feet slipping in the scree, there is good humor and excitement. When the edit cuts to the long shot of the mountain and the slope you hear an audible gasp from those in the gallery, engrossed in the spectacle.

The communal experience of viewing these scenes sets it apart from an encounter on a website. In the gallery space at the Biennale, people turn to each other. We are all witnessing something special here and imagine what will happen when the summit is reached. Before the children get there, we hear singing and try to make it out. Only afterwards do we learn it is a song which celebrates the boys conquering the mountain, conquering the mine which looms large over them. So, what does happen at the end of the struggle? The boy climbs into the tire, tucks himself right in, and sets the tire in motion, all the way back down, at high speed. With no little risk to life and limb, he hurtles down the slope. In the gallery, some of the viewers put their hands over their mouths in amazement. More than one looks at a child they have with them and wonders if it will ever try anything like that.

There are more questions than answers here. It is a game, but it is also free play, unbound and lost in the moment. The danger here is palpable: broken bones, concussion, something even more serious. The people watching are gripped, particularly by the shots from inside the tire. What will happen at the end of the ride? Will the boy be unharmed? As the tire rolls to a halt and falls over, the boy clambers out, a little unsteadily but without any obvious injury. These events are taking place in the epicenter of the developed world's quest for natural resources to meet its urgent digital demands. The waste from the vast cobalt mine below is the daily backdrop to their lives. Yet the tire and the song of victory over the mine are also a commandeering by the children of their local environment, of the resource and affordance in the landscape. They set up an experience fashioned from waste and expedience that has key features in common with other forms of play. Because, what happens next? The boy more or less immediately starts to clamber back up the slope to go again. Play is repetitive as well as environmentally specific. Where we do not always see it, children do almost always see possibility in their immediate location: the affordances of the tire and a steep mountain of mining waste, the effort of the long climb pushing it up and the payback, the thrill of the ride down inside it. The edit of the film switches between scale and struggle, between adrenaline and triumph, between breathlessness and sound. It is childhood in action, agency, and affect. It is hardly the trivial, the ephemeral. The film is steeped in action and operates at huge scale.

III

I move on through the exhibition and discover *Children's Game #25: Contagio* (2021) from Malinalco in Mexico. An establishing shot sets the scene, with distant mountains, a barking dog, and clotheslines hanging in a cobbled streetscape. Two children enter the frame. They wear black face masks, bump elbows, and run with others towards the location of the game, a dusty play space. A child enters the center of the shot with her back turned away from the others and begins the countdown to the start of the game. She is wearing a red face mask denoting herself as the chaser, the one with the 'contagion,' the COVID-19 virus. As she chases the others you can see that the rules allow children to be safe if they are off the ground, on or touching a stone, but only for a short, counted-out period of time. As more and more of the children don a red scarf after being tagged and are, therefore, 'infected,' the winner emerges as one of the girls, the last one standing. She climbs on a stone and announces that she is a survivor. All the remaining children applaud. Viewers in the gallery connect with the many variations of the tagging and chasing game worldwide and, of course, with the COVID-19 emergency.

This game, I realize, is of particular interest to me since it reminds me of a project I have been involved with in recent years. My *Play Observatory* colleagues and I have collected instances of children's play during the various COVID-19 lockdowns. Working entirely online during the pandemic, we have invited parents, caregivers, and children to send us examples of lockdown play in the form of videos, images, sounds, or text. As a UK-funded project, the emphasis was on the state of play during COVID-19 in our own country, but we also received examples from further afield and drawn from across the age range, from the very young to late teens. Our aim was twofold. Firstly, we wanted to archive the submissions as examples of experiences in a specific set of historical circumstances for future generations to explore. Secondly, we wanted

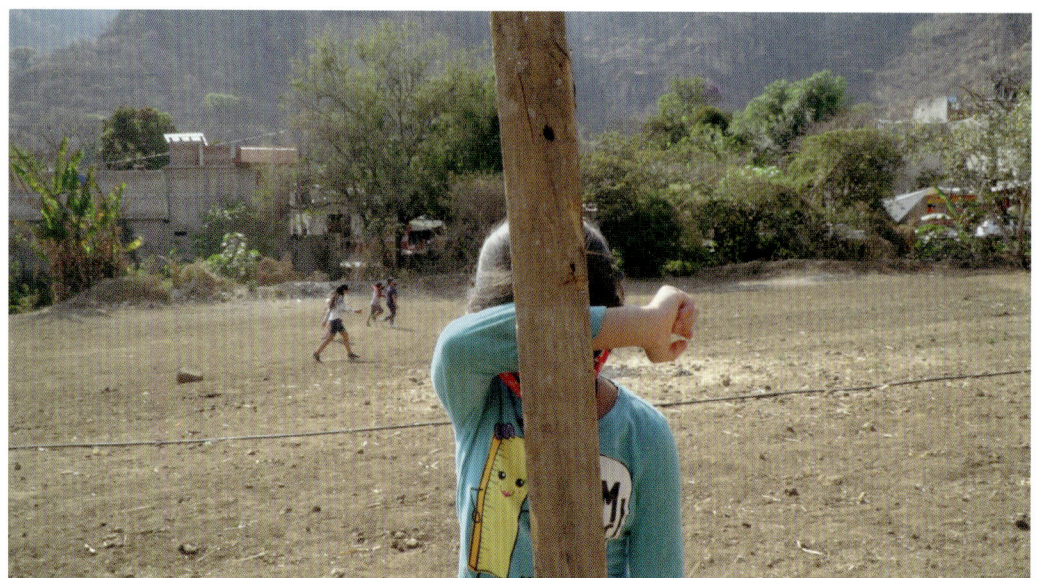

Francis Alÿs, *Children's Game #25: Contagio*, Malinalco, Mexico, 2021 (still)

to document them in the 'here and now' as a piece of social science research, and to represent lockdown play in an online exhibition in collaboration with the Victoria and Albert Museum's Young V&A team.[4]

Contagio makes me think of one of the folklorists and archivists on our team, Julia Bishop, who has been writing about variants of 'Corona Tag' which she had been finding and cataloguing. These are chasing games with the added danger of being touched by whoever was the chaser, and 'catching the virus.'[5] We had found versions of this game which children were banned from playing due to fears about COVID-19 infection before it was widely understood to be largely airborne in transmission. With customary resourcefulness in one case, children continued to play the game but tagged each other by touching their shadows. Dealing with fear, as well as playing risky games, in a community setting reinforces connection and cultural continuity. We saw this connectivity also in clapping games we researched in pre-COVID-19 times in an earlier project.[6] In one of our papers from research in the *Play Observatory* we have written about how

> …despite appearing new, with their timely renaming, games such as 'coronavirus tag' build on much older themes in play. Folklorists have noted that 'plague' and 'fever' were widespread names for chasing games during the twentieth century, with associated rituals for in-game immunity, such as crossing fingers or covering mouths …. More recently, and in digital form, contagion and survival have been central themes in a number of videogames released prior to the pandemic such as *Resident Evil*, *Halo* and *Plague Inc*. Play is therefore a complex intertwining of contemporary influences and longer histories and traditions …[7]

Alÿs has also spoken of the ways in which children are connected to larger, sometimes traumatic events and how they process them by altering forms of play. He challenges the notion of a state of childhood as a state of 'disconnection,' particularly in relation to the pandemic. In an interview about *The Nature of the Game* he says that "to think that children are disconnected is wrong, they're actually very affected and connected and trying to make sense of what's happening around them."[8]

It is possible to see community and connection as major themes in *The Nature of the Game*. These subjects become palpable when children take control of an immediate environment and prepare a space to communicate and exchange cultural information. It is present, for example, in the communal effort required to set up the game of *Kisolo*, once again in the Democratic Republic of the Congo. Children dig in the hard, sandy soil, organize the pieces, and gather the players together (*Children's Game #26: Kisolo* (2021)). We see it also in the glances between the girls who play *Jump Rope* in Hong Kong, against the backdrop of the urban skyline and the ochre terrace which becomes a small, local play space (*Children's Game #22: Jump Rope* (2020)). The filming and editing emphasize connection by swapping focus on each of the girls in turn. The soundtrack is the faint click of the rope on the ground, the words spoken between them, and their laughter as the game intensifies and the speed increases. The video ends when the camera pans up the nearest tower block and we see how Hong Kong looms over them. We appreciate how they have temporarily owned the space. Back in the Democratic Republic of the Congo again, we also see community and culture in the shared gazes and movement in *Children's Game #28: Nzango* (2021) as the girls trade and mirror dance moves which are impossible to follow unless you are in the know. We find it in Belgium in *Children's Game #31: Slakken* (2021), the game with snails where the space is carefully marked out and owned. The shared knowledge of the environment shapes the interactions. And in the snowy play of *Children's Game #33: Schneespiele* (2022) in Switzerland, anarchy regularly threatens, the whole experience teetering on the brink of collapse. It never actually does, however, as community and connection reestablish themselves.

While many games in the exhibition take place in specific kinds of play spaces – readily available or created in bespoke fashion by the players in the environment – one of the games invites us to join a trip through the city of Hong Kong. A girl makes her way across busy urban spaces and plays *Step on a Crack*. She uses her skill and the resource of the city itself (*Children's Game #23: Step on a Crack* (2020)). We are in October 2020, in pandemic times. The girl is wearing a mask, but this girl is confidently out and about, not stepping on any cracks or painted street signs on the floor of the city. The film locates her skipping apparently effortlessly through, then loses her, and finds her again, as do the spectators who are on the ground in Hong Kong, skillfully woven into the edit. This game is, at first glance, an individual experience of wayfaring, travelling on invisible paths through the space. Yet at second glance we see that the city itself is also joining in with the reaction of spectators who have their own negotiations with space in the busy and kaleidoscopic city. She chants as she goes, her words lost at times in the sound of road diggers and jackhammers, just as her movement is obscured by the traffic which pulls in in front of the camera. The editing and the language of the moving image guide us towards the idea of a single, unbroken 'journey as game.' Interestingly, this game mirrors the process of the margin becoming the center within *The Nature of the Game* itself.

Alÿs has spoken of how he initially intended this piece to be a portrait of the city of Hong Kong at a particular moment in time:

> The action itself was a pretext so that people would look at the city behind, and the life of the city, in this case, at a particular moment of its history, but it was a way of creating ambulation, a journey, through a place, and to portrait it, but without making it the first protagonist. … This was the intention. It turned out that the girl was quite charismatic, and she takes a lot of presence and that, in many ways, is the way I work.[9]

In the film, the girl stitches the scenes together, along with the city itself, in her movement through the space. Yet, interestingly, in both her confident, playful pathfinding and the reflected gaze of the spectators, she continually becomes the central subject of the film: her game, in her city, at this particular moment in time.

IV

After the show, I watched some of these games on the website. Online, the first few seconds of each game play out on a grid, with each moving thumbnail underscored by a location, a year, and an interpretation. In the gallery space, in the light of the monumental screens, you encounter first and foremost the games themselves. The where and when of each game are only gleaned by accessing the panel at the side of the displays. Only after having watched the video can you take your eyes off the action for long enough to dispel the initial rapture and remember that this is an exhibition. You then realize that you must do the things you usually do in a gallery: observe, read, think.

Watching the videos again on the website made me reflect on the route I took while visiting *The Nature of the Game*. I doubled back so many times to *La roue*, *Imbu* and *Step on a Crack* that I do not know whether I was really supposed to follow a line. I was, perhaps, wayfaring through the displays of the games, retracing and pausing, re-visiting, and then sometimes stopping to share the experience with remote *Play Observatory* colleagues via my phone. For some of the visitors it seemed to be enough to wander in briefly and then to re-emerge into the light of the Giardini. For others there was a pause and chance to recalibrate their understanding of certain key features of children's games, drawn from cultural memory or encountering something new. This experience is no mere triviality. Children's games, along with their play, are not an abandoned extra at the margin of human experience. Every day, in every space – poor, rich, hot, cold, in a conflict, overcrowded, dwarfed by the size and shape of a space – there are children playing. Sometimes the games they play are rule-bound in the loosest, simplest sense. Others are driven by a complex negotiation with a set of fixed rules and rituals. Sometimes these games happen in the very direst of human experience. In every case, they seem to lose their players to the flow, in the movement, and in the gaze of friends and strangers alike, so that the past is in the present and the future is the undiscovered space out of view.

The Nature of the Game opens the possibility that childhood is at the center of a set of important lived experiences instead of being lost at the margins. It also reminds us that children are alive in the moment. They are fully formed in the instant of play and negotiation. They are not only in a state of 'becoming' but are also 'being,' as the new childhood studies tell us.[10] In the apparently trivial but ultimately complex in-game negotiations taking place from moment to moment lies the possibility of making the world anew each time, with a focus on empathy, communication, and shared experience.

Though filmed and edited by adults, *The Nature of the Game* manages to capture the child-led version of childhood. Seldom do these players look up from their games. There are no adults around to enforce rules. Those who are in the films are going about their own business or spectating at the margins, occasionally talking with one another. The girl in Hong Kong has a brief look and lowers her mask at the end of *Step on a Crack*, but in most other cases children are lost in the flow, locked into codes and conventions in their own ecosystem. Perhaps this sense of performance out of adult reach, though recorded and observed, arises from the circumstances in which the project began. Alÿs has explained that over a number of years the filming of these games was tangential to his own main projects.[11] Over time it moved from the margins of his work into the center.

The Nature of the Game reconnects our present and future with our past as players, as children, as people who shared spaces and experiences with one another. "We were small," writes Seamus Heaney, thinking of himself and his playmates, "and thought we knew nothing worth knowing."[12] This exhibition underlines, however, that these games *are* worth knowing. They put us at the center of something both lost and found. 'Lost' because of the sedimentation of adulthood which accumulates through time, obscures memory, and relegates play in importance as we get older and, in some cases, the struggle for survival takes over. 'Lost' also because of the lack of attention that is paid to the ostensibly trivial, with play being made inaccessible and community, and connection, being easily forgotten. Yet 'found' because of work like *The Nature of the Game*, which does not comment but situates each game in its own space. It invites the viewer to be drawn into those games, to both value them for their own sake and appreciate how they can be documented and brought to life. We need the ingenuity, the resourcefulness, the invention, and the connection to each other which games reveal more than ever in a world beset by conflict and climate disaster. *The Nature of the Game* draws us back to the possibility of negotiation and community, to shared culture and connection. In a world which is arguably in thrall to individual wealth and attainment, the games remind us of other ways of being that we once knew and would do well to find again.

Notes

1. Francis Alÿs (2022). *Francis Alÿs Publications: Children's Games.* Retrieved October 10, 2022, from http://francisalys.com/category/childrens-games/

2. Alÿs (2022). Op. cit.

3. Sonia Boyce (2022). *Feeling Her Way.* British Council, Venice Biennale. https://venicebiennale.britishcouncil.org/feeling-her-way

4. Our website and the exhibition are still available to view, and we are currently engaged in general dissemination, giving talks, and writing papers. Kate Cowan, John Potter, Yinka Olusoga, Catherine Bannister, Julia C. Bishop, Michelle Cannon, & Valerio Signorelli (2021). "Children's Digital Play during the COVID-19 Pandemic: insights from the Play Observatory." *Journal of e-Learning and Knowledge Society,* *17*(3), 8–17; YoungV&A, Episod_Studio, & The_Play_Observatory (2022). *Play in the Pandemic.* https://playinthepandemic.play-observatory.com.

5. Anna Beresin & Julia Bishop (eds.) (2023). *Play in a Covid Frame: Everyday Pandemic Creativity in a Time of Isolation.* OBP (Open Books Publisher). https://doi.org/10.11647/OBP.0326.

6. John Potter & Kate Cowan (2020). "Playground as meaning-making space: Multimodal making and re-making of meaning in the (virtual) playground." *Global Studies of Childhood, 10*(3), 248–263.

7. Cowan et. al. (2021). Op. cit.

8. Jurrell Lewis (July 2022). Francis Alÿs discusses *The Nature of the Game* in the 2022 Venice Biennale "The Milk of Dreams." Art21. https://art21.org/read/in-the-studio-francis-alys/. Our *Play Observatory* project certainly accords with this view. The online exhibition of work contains many examples of children demonstrating affect and connection in different ways during their lockdown play. YoungV&A et. al. (2022). Op. cit.

9. Alÿs in Lewis (July 2022). Op. cit.

10. See, for example, Allison James (2009). "Agency." In: Jens Qvortrup, William A. Corsaro, & Michael Sebastian Honig (eds.), *The Handbook of Childhood Studies.* London: Palgrave Macmillan. 34–45. In the *Play Observatory*, we found that paying attention to play, rather than 'learning loss,' was key to learning more about children's experiences during the pandemic. We continue to be concerned with speaking back to power about how children were living during these times.

11. Lewis (July 2022). Op. cit.

12. "The Railway Children" in Seamus Heaney (1984). *Station Island.* London: Faber.

,

Sharing the Game

Giulio Piovesan*

I

Working as an exhibition attendant, one has great advantage over everyone else, over the curator of the show, or over the artist whose works are being shown. Whoever happens to hold this position has the chance to spend weeks or months in front of a painting, side by side with a sculpture, immersed in a site-specific installation. Eventually they will gain an insight into the exhibition of a different nature than the knowledge which proceeds from academic research or from having created an artwork with one's own bare hands. What an exhibition attendant acquires over the course of time is a vast array of information that can very seldom be surmised before a show opens to the public and begins existing in ways that its artist and its curator might not even have imagined.

The most obvious thing that one tries to assess right from the start is how long the display is going to last, if it will withstand the wear of time and the passing through of the visitors. It is essential to estimate as early as possible what is likely to malfunction, suffer damages, or be stolen. Such awareness helps prevent accidents and keep the exhibition a tight compound of form and content. However, that condition pertains to the world of physics and practicalities. In due time, further considerations will come up in the mind of the exhibition attendant: considerations that arise only if one spends a significant number of hours inside a given space, watching the same video installation hundreds of times, or

* Giulio Piovesan is an Italian journalist and photographer. He worked as an exhibition attendant for *Francis Alÿs. The Nature of the Game*, presented at the Belgian pavilion during the 59th Venice Biennale from April 23 until November 27, 2022.

looking at a sculpture from all available viewpoints and in all imaginable light conditions; considerations that are the products of personal observations and of interactions with the visitors. Indeed, after a few weeks of working at an exhibition, one forges a bond with it, and the visitors offer a good buffer to their reading of the project and of its execution.

So, although nowadays people who visit an exhibition certainly do not have much time to spend with its staff – because they want to see as much as possible before closing time – they are so many as to provide an endless stream of feedback. It is by conversing with visitors and by entertaining personal, often unuttered, speculations that the exhibition attendant is in a position to attempt to answer a number of questions which should never vacate the rooms of contemporary art. *Will this artwork still be topical in the future? Is it intelligible to the general public? Does it speak to the global community or only to the people living in this part of the world? Does it lend itself to the superimposition of new layers of meaning? Is it food for thought or just one more item of contemporary art toying with many visitors' constant search for cheap fun?*

II

In 2022, I worked as an exhibition attendant for about seven months at Francis Alÿs's *The Nature of the Game*. For 32 weeks – that is, for the whole duration of his participation in the 59th edition of Venice Biennale – I experienced the impact of his video installation, on myself and on the visitors. For six days per week, eight hours per day, my eyes were filled with moving images of children playing street games in different countries, from Belgium to the Democratic Republic of the Congo, from Mexico to Hong Kong, by way of Switzerland and Afghanistan. I saw them play alone, in small or large groups. In summer, in winter, in cities, in villages. I heard them sing, whisper, laugh, scream. And so did

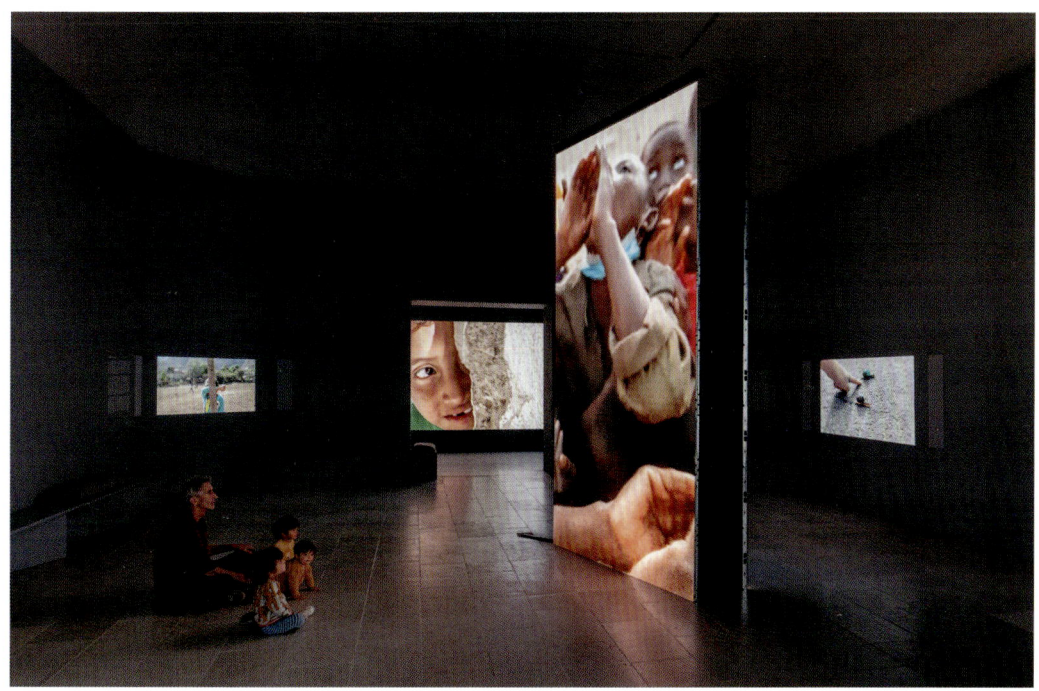

Installation view *Francis Alÿs. The Nature of the Game*, Belgian pavilion, 59th Venice Biennale (2022) (photo by Roberto Ruiz)

the visitors – people of all ages and walks of life, each of them carrying their own expectations and biases. They were a multitude: over 800,000 individuals, 35 percent more than the attendance of the previous edition of the Biennale. This increase meant that every day an average of 4,000 people visited Alÿs's exhibition, making it the most successful art project ever hosted by the Belgian pavilion.

Yet it was not simply a matter of figures. For even though nowadays most of the art world shares the entertainment industry's craving for a new record in ticket sales or for the widest media coverage, the real success of an exhibition should be measured by the impact it has on people, by how it affects them and makes them leave with a different attitude toward the issues it calls attention to. It most definitely has something to do with the artist's ability to stir people's emotions, but also with their ability to stimulate people's minds as well. That is exactly what Alÿs did with *The Nature of the Game*. He aroused feelings and thoughts, he made visitors react on different levels, from the emotional to the intellectual. He succeeded in dragging them into a visual and aural playground, making them feel as if they were popping their heads out of their windows to peer down at the children playing in the backyard. Perhaps distractedly at first, but then with wonder and amusement.

Sometimes matters of fact become apparent through minor details. In the case of *The Nature of the Game,* the sheer number of visitors was documented by the doormat at the entrance of the pavilion. It was made of grey PVC, and at the shop where it was bought they said it would last forever. Indeed, it survived four editions of the Biennale, but in 2022 it fell victim to the 800,000 pairs of feet that walked on it. Every evening, at closing time, I used to pull it in to shut the main door. For the first few weeks it let itself be drawn in, without showing any sign of premature aging. Then, in the summer, I noticed that when I pulled it in, it presented a rip near its middle, a short cut that started from its edge along the front steps and aimed at its center. After further inspection, I also noticed that the whole doormat was quite worn-out and that its texture was fraying. With each passing day, I saw it steadily deteriorate, much faster than it had done in the previous years. I saw it become thinner and thinner while the cut progressed toward its center. So much so that during the last weeks of the Biennale every time that I pulled it in, it almost split in half and eventually, when the exhibition was over, it had to be disposed of. At first, I thought that they had lied at the shop, that the doormat was made of a poor-quality material. Then, though, I realized that it was just bearing witness to what I could see with my own eyes: an unprecedented number of visitors coming and going the whole time. Even in the middle of summer, when the attendance usually drops before rising again in September, I was aware that never before had I seen so many people crossing the threshold of the pavilion.

Yet there was something that puzzled me. Although being there for 54 hours per week would have been tiring for anybody, and I have never liked being stuck in packed places, the crowd visiting *The Nature of the Game* did not bother me that much. It did not annoy me as it had in the past. Nobody complained and nobody ever left in a hurry because they thought that the show was a rip-off. Actually, almost everybody watched all the videos in their entirety. Many stood in front of the screens, others sat on the benches or even on the floor. Some people started watching the short movies and waited for a *coup de théâtre* to happen, confident that the installation could not possibly be just about children playing street games. Then, it suddenly dawned on them that it really was about kids playing in streets and village yards. As soon as they realized that, their faces relaxed and their bodies loosened up, as if they had finally reached a place free of adult nonsense. I have a vivid memory of a young girl, aged 25 or so. At first, she looked around in disbelief, but then I saw a flash of recognition on her face as her expression of perplexity turned into a smile. She got it! I did not know what exactly, but she got it. She grasped something or perhaps something hit her unexpectedly. It does not matter whether her reaction to the videos was rational or emotional, if she understood them or felt them. What matters is that she established a connection with them and responded to them, as any exhibition-goer happens to do whenever they are in front of an artwork gifted with the power to speak multiple languages. Indeed, almost everybody reacted to Alÿs's video installation, and everybody did it in their own way. That explains why, despite the large turnout of the Biennale of 2022, I was not bothered by the public and nobody took it out on me: everyone felt a sense of fulfillment because they had finally found an exhibition that spoke to each of them.

III

When visitors have something to complain about, they make sure that the exhibition attendant knows about it. Their ways of expressing their disapproval of a show range between the classic U-turn in the middle of the main room followed by an indignant walk toward the exit to real acts of physical assault. Anything between the two extremes is possible: arguing for half an hour, shouting abuse, scribbling insults in the visitor book, leaving rubbish behind, damaging the artworks, demanding to speak with the curator or to have one's ticket refunded. *The Nature of the Game* spared me all of that. It did so for a simple reason: it reached out to the public, and as a result the public did not have the bad feelings that come with an exhibition that one is not able to make sense of. It did not require people to do anything except watch, yet it seeped into them, triggering emotions, recollections, dormant musings. Which is what most individuals expect from an art exhibition. They – we – want to be engaged, in one way or another. In order to do so, the work of an artist must possess a distinctively human quality: it has to be forthcoming, like a person who is not just approachable by strangers but rather moves in their direction to connect with them.

Every accomplished artist achieves such a goal in their own way. Some artists build huge installations that in their still silence extend invisible antennae which take hold of the people around them and attract them as if they were magnets. Others, like Alÿs, produce artworks that run toward people and hold their attention until they have finished telling their story. Like children do when they want to share their findings with an adult. Indeed, one of the many things that I noticed during my seven-month immersion in *The Nature of the Game* was that the visitors of the show watched the videos with the same attitude that they might have had if they had been listening to a story told by their own children. They were fascinated by the simplicity of the games played by the young performers, and in that very simplicity they perceived something unmarred by the preoccupations of the grown-ups. A sort of truth that could be grasped by anybody, if only they still had the candor of a child. What I saw in many people's eyes was not the longing for the good old times when they played in the streets with their friends. They certainly had that feeling, but it also seemed that they were trying to decipher the single story that ran through all the videos, that truth or state of mind that escaped them, yet was within reach of kids who probably did not even attend school.

Of course, I might have misinterpreted people's facial expressions. Perhaps they were not looking for anything and they just happened to enjoy the videos. One sure thing is that many of them spent a long time inside the pavilion. That is quite unusual at the Biennale, since there are a lot of exhibits to see and people tend to rush not to miss a thing. After all, it is an all-you-can-eat event, and everybody wants to gorge on contemporary art before leaving. That is why I was so surprised to see that an unexpected number of visitors spent over one hour shifting from screen to screen and often double-checked to assure themselves that they had watched all the videos. Then there were those who left and would come back a few hours later to take another peek. A middle-aged man came in three times, while several small children tried to drag their parents into the pavilion every time they passed in front of it and were reminded of the show by the red ball that Alÿs had positioned above the main entrance's stone frame.

Everybody had their own favorite video, one which they felt a personal connection with or which they found most engaging. A video titled *Children's Game #29: La roue* (2021) attracted crowds of people in front of the screen. It documented a small Congolese child pushing a truck tire onto the top of a hill of mining debris and then tucking himself inside it to roll down the slope for pure fun. When the tire came to a stop at the foot of the waste hill, he would push it back onto the top of it and start his game again. Some visitors wondered how he managed to do that without breaking his neck; all of them watched with transport, raptured by how he turned the disheartening Western civilization's myth of Sisyphus into a game for the children of the Global South.

Indeed, quite a number of people were carried away by the children's ability to make do without actual toys and to upend the world of the adults. In *Children's Game #25: Contagio* (2021), for instance, a group of young Mexican boys and girls found a way to have fun with their own version of the COVID-19 pandemic. One of them was supposed to have an imaginary disease and in order to get rid of it he or she had to chase the others and touch someone else to pass it on. Whoever happened to be the chaser had to wear a red face mask. Those who watched the video could not but be reminded of one of the most basic, age-old games, yet they were surprised by how a pandemic that kept the world's population in a state of isolation was reimagined by a group of children as a way to be together. Another favorite video was titled *Children's Game #31: Slakken* (2021) and documented a group of Belgian children racing snails in the street. In a world where everything, from commodities to information, is expected to travel as fast as possible, those children were enthralled by one of the slowest animals on earth. Moreover, since the snails would not move in a straight line, they were positioned inside a

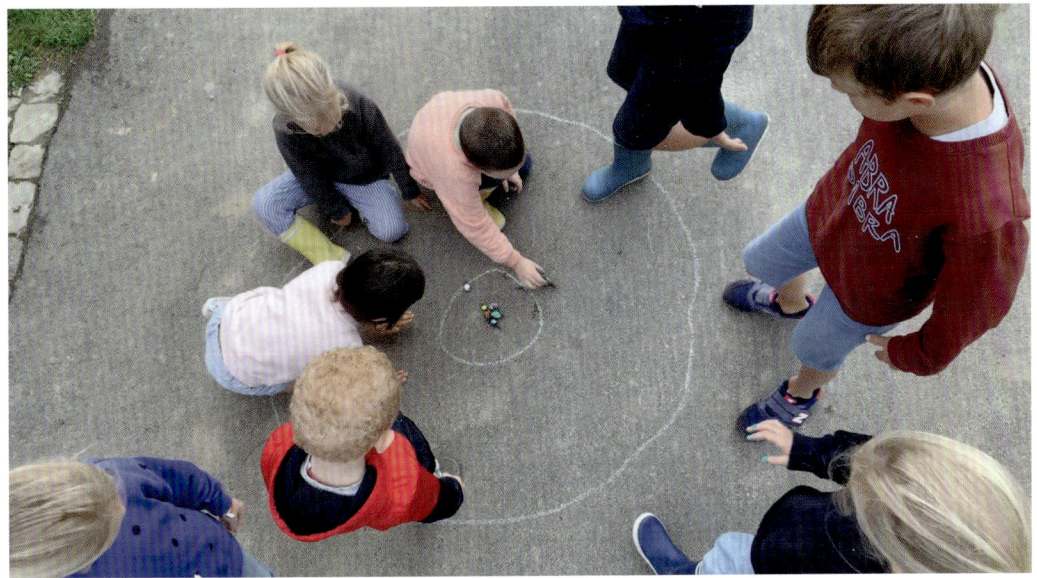

Francis Alÿs, *Children's Game #31: Slakken*, Pajottenland, Belgium, 2021 (still)

circle chalked on the pavement, and the winner would be the first one to cross the line. Each could go its own way, working with its young racer to show the grown-ups that everybody can find their own personal path to liberation.

Then there was a video which caused a woman to react very emotionally, as if it had pierced through all her intellectual filters and aroused some very intense memory buried deep within her. The video was titled *Children's Game #23: Step on a Crack* (2020) and showed a small girl playing alone in the busy streets and alleys of Hong Kong. She leapt forward and hopped left and right trying to avoid the cracks in the pavement or the gaps between the concrete slabs, arguably with the intent to bypass anything that disrupted the seamless urban route to her final destination. One day I was sitting on a bench, watching *Step on a Crack* for the umpteenth time, when an elderly woman and her husband sat right in front of the LED wall and started watching the video. After a short time, I turned toward the couple and noticed that the woman was crying, while her husband kept his hand on her shoulder as if to comfort her. Yet the man's expression was that of someone knowing that even though the person with them is in emotional distress, everything is fine and their reaction is just a human response to something that has stirred their deepest emotions. So, I wondered why his wife was crying, what feelings had been awakened by the video in front of her. Perhaps she was reminded of a daughter or of a granddaughter she had not seen in person for a long time, or someone she had lost. Or maybe she recollected her own childhood, when she might have played exactly the same game, as oblivious of the world and of history as the little girl from Hong Kong was seventy years after her. I could not know if her tears were of grief, nostalgia, or relief. All I knew was that she would be fine because her husband was with her and he would provide all the support she might need. What mattered most to me was that an artwork had affected a visitor in a way that I had never witnessed before – and that very likely I shall never witness again. *Step on a Crack* whispered into that woman's ear and tugged at her heartstrings, strings which probably had been untouched for decades and finally reverberated thanks to a work of contemporary art. If it is true, as some say, that real art has the power to cure, what artwork could cure a person better than one that speaks to them as candidly as a child and helps them release their most tangled, pent-up emotions?

IV

In addition to the positive feedback from the visitors, there was a further factor that proved how well-received *The Nature of the Game* was: the astonishing number of catalogs sold during the Biennale, both at the pavilion and at the bookshops. The book was a bestseller, so much so that it was constantly sold out and copies of it had to be sourced from any available stock. It was in such a high demand that not only the publisher, but also distributors and retailers based in various European countries had to hand over all their copies in order to meet the requests in Venice. The catalog was tiny, since it was a facsimile of Alÿs's pocket sketchbooks. It contained notes in different languages, drawings of the children playing the games in the videos, studies for the small oil paintings that were exhibited in the rooms by the entrance of the pavilion. It never failed to attract the visitors, who went through it with the same sense of wonder that they felt when watching the videos. They were certainly captivated by Alÿs's drawing skills, but what they appreciated most was that he had decided to share with them what he had seen during his many journeys, revealing how any inconspicuous detail can catch his attention and fuel his creative mind. So, quite a number of visitors browsed the catalog as if they were tiptoeing into his studio, or rather as if they were beside him while he took visual notes of a street scene that would eventually develop into one of his artworks. They knew that they were made privy to that moment when an artist translates the world into their own language; that moment which cannot be framed and hanged on a wall, being made of raw material which not even the artist has fully processed yet.

Indeed, the reason why in 2022 the visitors of the Biennale did not take it out on me or harass me with petty complaints, but rather had an urge to let me know how much they appreciated the exhibition, was that they felt relieved because they finally found an art installation and a catalog that spoke to them with no intellectual barriers. Never before had I been approached by so many people who wanted to express not just how much they liked the exhibition, but also their gratitude for having been offered an art project that did not communicate in an unnecessarily overcomplicated language. They were grateful for having been granted access into the world of an artist that shared his vision with them and talked to them in a straightforward manner. As directly and candidly as children do.

Illustration Credits

All images are courtesy of the artists.

Acknowledgements

The editors would like to give special thanks to:

Francis Alÿs and his team, Alessandra Biscaro, Geert Bouckaert, Elizabeth Calzado Michel, John Eyck, Miguel González Virgen, Leuven University Press, Jan Mot, Rafael Ortega, Bart Raymaekers, Luc Sels, Dirk Snauwaert, Hilde Teerlinck, Waseem Akhtar Usmani, Ester Van Ackere, Demmy Verbeke, Anne Verbrugge, Eva Wittocx, and all contributing authors.